FIGHTER JETS
READY-TO-BUILD-AND-FLY
MODEL AIRCRAFT

*With thanks to Clay Dearman and Less Wilkerson,
and especially to my wife, Terri.*

FIGHTER JETS
READY-TO-BUILD-AND-FLY
MODEL AIRCRAFT

CURTIS L. BOYLL

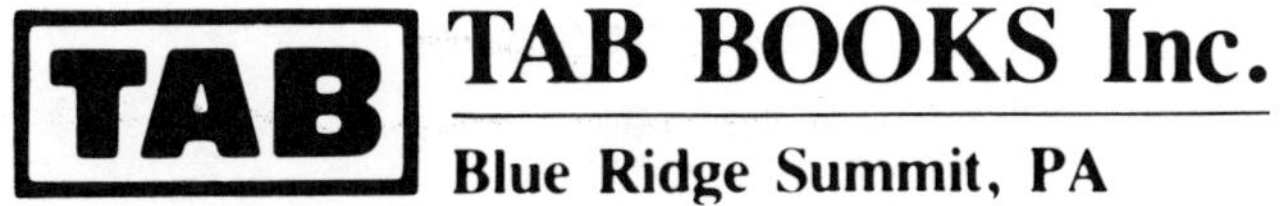

TAB BOOKS Inc.

Blue Ridge Summit, PA

FIRST EDITION
SECOND PRINTING

Library of Congress Cataloging in Publication Data

Boyll, Curtis L.
Fighter jets : ready-to-build-and-fly model aircraft / by Curtis
L. Boyll.
p.   cm.
ISBN 0-8306-2967-X (pbk.)
1. Jet planes, Military—Models.   I. Title.

TL770.B63   1988
629.133′ 1349—dc19   87-34483
                                                    CIP

TAB BOOKS Inc. offers software for
sale. For information and a catalog,
please contact TAB Software Department,
Blue Ridge Summit, PA 17294-0850.

Questions regarding the content of this book
should be addressed to:

Reader Inquiry Branch
TAB BOOKS Inc.
Blue Ridge Summit, PA 17294-0214

Contents

Introduction

THERE IS GREAT PUBLIC AWARENESS OF THE NATURE OF WEAPONS AND combat vehicles. There is a resurging popularity of military air shows, as well as visits aboard battleships and aircraft carriers. With the precedent of American history, it is appropriate for Americans to know about the weapons and vehicles that help preserve freedom, and also those that would end it.

The introduction of cardstock model aircraft is a response to these growing interests of the public. This is a series of standoff-scale model aircraft that are assembled from cardstock and that fly comparable to existing hand-launched gliders of many types. The eight 1/81st standoff-scale models in this volume include jet fighters used by various countries, including the United States, France, and the Soviet Union.

Hand-launched gliders provide the light exercise and fun recreation of flying model airplanes, both indoors and out. Flying scale models can fulfill a role similar to the civilian spotting manuals used 30 years ago. Cardstock model aircraft are intended to be more effective and useful in familiarizing the general public than spotting manuals could ever be because the actual aircraft shapes are much more explicit in model form, and watching the aircraft flying can be much more realistic than pictures in a spotting manual.

A Brief History

THE HISTORY OF TURBINE-ENGINE-POWERED, OR *JET* COMBAT AIRCRAFT began only recently, with the entirety of it contained within the time since the last world war. Actually, the very earliest jet fighters flew during World War II, including the German Me-262 and the British Gloster Meteor. The first operational American jet fighter, the Lockheed F-80 Shooting Star, was first flown in 1944 and was put into service just after the war.

With the defeat of Hitler and the Japanese, American efforts pioneered the way to high-performance aircraft, and in 1947 the experimental Bell X-1 achieved flight beyond the speed of sound. The first use of jet fighter aircraft in large-scale combat occurred during the American involvement as a United Nations force in Korea. Later, American forces relied on the F-105 Thunderchief and the famed F-4 Phantoms in the skies over Vietnam. Both of these are among the very first operational supersonic fighters from the United States.

In modern 'limited' wars, the use of jet fighters, instead of large bombers, is the norm. They have been used effectively in conflicts in Egypt, the Falklands, and Afghanistan, and in the civil war in Lebanon—situations that have required combat aircraft to perform many different roles.

Modern technological advances have led to the design and operational use of ever more potent weapons carried by ever more powerful and sophisticated aircraft, with electronics increasing the capabilities of aircraft while reducing size and weight. This has brought about the advent of the *multirole fighter*, a jet fighter that can do many different jobs. This jet can fly very fast and carry missiles as an interceptor; it is very maneuverable, able to fly long distances patrolling borders; it can take the fight to the enemy by carrying tons of bombs and dropping them accurately; or it can do all of these things on a single mission, in the case of a few designs.

The modern multirole fighter is a formidable weapons system, able to perform a wide variety of combat missions in a nation's defense if and when required. In a time of deterrence through bombers, missiles, and submarines, jet fighters still perform a much more important role in all nations than was once envisioned.

For many small countries, the economics and logistics of jet fighters are very appealing compared to other, far more complex and expensive weapons systems. The proven flexibility of fighter aircraft enables them to perform many different tasks, and this saves money and manpower. Because they are less expensive than alternatives, larger numbers can be produced and deployed. Force of numbers has always been important in warfare.

Suggested Tools

EVEN THOUGH THE MODELS ARE SOMETIMES COMPLEX IN SHAPE, THE patterns make it easy to construct each cardstock model aircraft from only a few parts. Construction is much easier than that for nonflying plastic models, and the resulting gliders resemble the full-scale aircraft to a much greater degree than traditional low-cost balsa flying models. Consisting of typically only six parts, most models can be assembled in about an hour, even by those who have never enjoyed model airplanes. No special tools are needed besides scissors, a ballpoint pen, and a ruler or straightedge.

Plastic transparent mending tape is recommended, because glue has not been found to be as sturdy, nor as easy to use. Common scissors are easier and faster to use than razor blades or knives, and do not score the building surface. A hard, flat surface for assembly is very important to the flying characteristics of all the models.

In addition to the patterned parts included in this book, the only other requirements are at least one common paperclip per aircraft for proper balance; some models require two. Be sure to use a flat surface as much as possible during assembly, and use care so that the fuselage, wings, and tail are as properly aligned as possible.

Begin by studying the model parts and assembly drawings carefully. Before you start assembling any of the models, it is important that you be somewhat familiar with the way the models are presented. Read all of the *General Discussion* through before you start to build. After deciding which model to build first, also read the section of *Detailed Instructions* for that model before starting. This way you will be familiar with all of the steps before you begin, and you will find it easy to produce good-looking models.

Model Designs

BECAUSE ALL OF THE MODELS PRESENTED HAVE MANY COMMON FEAtures, this discussion summarizes typical construction techniques. In order to reduce the instructions required for building the models, all of the general aspects will be discussed here, and the specific details for each model will be provided later in brief, separate sections.

These cardstock model aircraft have been designed for great stability and ruggedness in order to provide lots of hand-launched flying fun. The models are very simple, yet some steps should be accomplished with care in order to provide the best in paper-airplane flying. Each has a main wing, fuselage (body), tail fin, horizontal stabilizer, and canopy. (Refer briefly to the actual drawings of parts for the models, provided on the heavier cardstock paper, and familiarize yourself with these basic parts of almost any airplane.)

Find the two pages of parts for the model you might like to build first, and follow this discussion using the drawings for that model. Remember, the order that the models are in does not indicate which to build first; it is merely the chronological order of deployment of the actual jet fighters. If any of the models could be considered a good first 'trainer', it might be the F-105 Thunderchief. This model is quite basic, representing just about the simplest form of all. The F-105 is very stable and easy to fly because of its somewhat larger size, and it is one of the most rugged models.

A Properly Built Wing

On sheet 'A' of each drawing, you will find the top view, side view, and front view. The wing and stabilizer for most models are provided on the top view drawing. The fuselage shown in the top view is not used in the actual model, and you must cut it away from the wing and stabilizer. The side and front views are also not used in the model. They are reference drawings, showing how the completed model should look.

Observe the wing and stabilizer in the top view. Notice the tabs added to the front of each part. The tabs along the wing, or *wing tabs*, give the wing the necessary strength and help to form the proper wing camber. Fold these tabs under the wing or stabilizer. They help reinforce the wing, as well as contribute to the airfoil shape. On some models, you will fold the wing tabs under the rear of the wing or stabilizer. Again, they add to the strength and the ruggedness of the model aircraft.

The wing of each model is the most important part. It is the wing that allows the model to fly, and several interesting aspects of the wing will be described later. You should take care when preparing the wing and the stabilizer to be sure that the parts are straight and flat, with no warping. If the wing is warped, it will severely affect the way in which the model flies, and this problem is difficult to correct after the model is completed.

<h1>Preparing the Fuselage</h1>

While the wing provides lift for the model to fly, it cannot do so if the tail surfaces are not fixed in the proper alignment. The *fuselage*, or body, of the model provides the strength for the model to withstand the forces of flight and of hard landings. A sturdy and rigid fuselage keeps the horizontal and vertical stabilizers in alignment, and is important in providing the ruggedness for hundreds of flights.

To form a typical fuselage, first roll the paper pattern around a large marker pen, or any other round rod or dowel about ½ inch thick. Once the fuselage is curled slightly in this manner, it is much easier to form the proper shape. Be careful not to crease the fuselage while rolling it into shape. Alignment marks are provided on the model parts. Use them to help get the fuselage correct quickly.

FIGURE 11 shows typical alignment marks. Use two small pieces of tape to lightly 'tack' the bottom of the fuselage together. After checking to make sure that the alignment is just right, add additional tape to hold the fuselage securely. The fuselage must not be twisted or bent, or the wing and stabilizer will not be aligned correctly. At least one model does not have a rounded fuselage, but a square one.

<h1>Advanced-Design Fuselage</h1>

Certain models have required more complexity in order to accommodate air intakes and provide greater strength. These models have three or four separate fuselage sections instead of just one, and their assembly is a bit more involved. The Russian Su-7 and MiG-21 models have special details for the nose, which provide the shape of a 'radar cone' within the center of the nose of the model. Parts provided for this are a cone-shaped center and an outer ring which secures it to the nose of the model. Not only does this make the model resemble the full-size fighter, it also makes its nose very sturdy.

The fuselage designs for the Etendard, the Phantom, and the Skyhawk are very different from the basic rolled tube. The *lateral intakes*, or intakes mounted on the sides, of these models are provided so that they closely resemble their full-size counterparts. These models have a fuselage made up of four separate parts: left and right front, and left and right rear components.

Advanced designs incorporate even greater strength than the simpler models, with better geometry and the use of the basic strengths of the materials. The fundamental ruggedness of the transparent tape and cardstock is based on the compression rigidity of the cardstock and the adhesive strength of the tape. The tape holds the paper in place to make the best use of the rigidity. The tape itself also can provide rigidity when used in layers. These two features are used in the more complex designs in such a way that the models are strongest along their length, and resist crushing or bending much more than simpler designs. Details of construction are provided later in the *Assembly Instructions*.

All of the models require you to make cuts at the nose and tail so that the fuselage tapers inward. This is where the appearance of the model can be sacrificed if you are not careful. Typically, you should completely cut away the black lines showing the tapered cuts so that they do not show on the completed model. Once cut out, simply bring the edges of these areas together and tape them one by one.

For the basic models, the final step in preparing the fuselage usually includes cutting slots for the wing and stabilizer. I recommend that you first pierce through the cardstock at the front of the line indicated, and then cut along the line toward the rear of the model. Making a rounded pierce at the front of the cut helps decrease the possibility of the slot tearing farther forward than it should under the stresses of hard landings. Take care to be sure that the slot lines are in proper alignment, which is determined by taping the fuselage together properly to begin with.

<h1>Aligning the Wing and Fuselage</h1>

One of the most important areas to observe is the angle of the stabilizer to the wing. When you are looking at the model fuselage from either side, the front of the stabilizer should not be angled upward relative to the main wing. When you hold the wing, or the slots for the wing, in a horizontal position, the stabilizer and its slots also should be horizontal, or pointed downward slightly at the front. Each model's tail design has this feature incorporated into it.

If the leading edge of the stabilizer is angled upward at all, it has what is called *positive angle of incidence* to the main wing, and this must be corrected. There is nothing that can be done for the model later that will cure the problems caused by positive incidence of the stabilizer. If, for any reason, the slot lines for the stabilizer appear to be angled upward relative to the wing, cut the slots slightly off the lines, so that the stabilizer is straight or angled slightly downward at the front. Due to design considerations, this should not be a problem, especially if you check it during the assembly of each model.

Mating the wing and fuselage involves inserting the wing through the slots cut for it, and achieving the proper alignment before you tape it into place. Lines drawn on the wing pattern indicate where to align the fuselage on the wing, and you should take care to be sure the wing stays in place while you are applying the tape. The summary at the end of the *Assembly Instructions* shows how to fold a crease in the tape to make it easier to attach the wing to the fuselage.

Assembling the Tail and Canopy

The horizontal stabilizer is attached in very much the same way as the wings, by inserting it through the slots near the rear of the fuselage. Again, be sure that the stabilizer is at the proper angle of incidence relative to the main wing.

One of the easiest parts to assemble and attach is the vertical stabilizer, also known as the *fin*. Bring the two halves of this part together and tape the edges securely. Then apply tape to the tabs provided, position the fin over the rear of the fuselage, and press the tabs down so that the tape fastens them onto the fuselage. Be sure the fin is not angled to either side before you tape it down securely.

The canopy for each model is usually assembled last. As for the fuselage, form the canopy into its proper shape by rolling it around a pen or pencil. Once curled into a rounded shape, it is much easier to fold the canopy together for the best scale appearance. Bring the edges of the front parts of the canopy together and tape in place. Then position the canopy over the fuselage, press down, and tape securely.

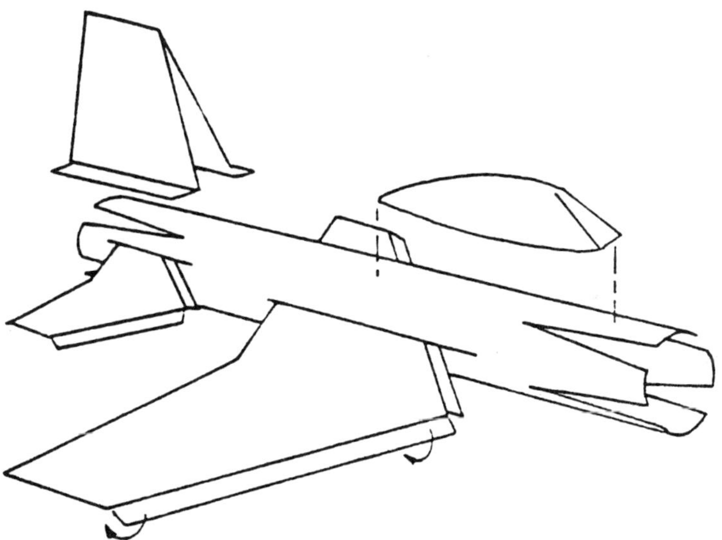

Fig. 1. This is an exploded view of a typical midwing model.

Flying Cardstock Models

DESIGNED AS SMALL HAND-LAUNCHED GLIDERS, CARDSTOCK MODEL AIR-craft are fast and rugged. All of the models behave somewhat alike, with better stability and more variety of maneuvers than simpler models provide. Even though cardstock is heavier than paper, these designs fly great because they take advantage of the more sophisticated aerodynamics of successful jet fighters. Cardstock is much stronger and more durable than paper, so each model can provide hundreds of flights.

Expect flights of a least 30 feet indoors, and much farther outdoors. Even though first attempts at building and flying might require minor adjustments, after you become familiar with the models, you will find that some fly quite well on their very first flight.

The basic principles of flight apply to these models just as they do for larger aircraft. The basics include the forces of thrust, drag, lift, and weight. The thrust provided by the hand launch must overcome the aerodynamic drag, and this drag will begin to slow the model after it is released. While moving forward through the air, the wing can provide the lift, which overcomes weight, allowing the model to fly. When drag slows the plane down, however, the wing can no longer produce enough lift and model descends. With the lift that the wing provides, these models have been flown to distances of over 100 feet, and have at times remained airborne for more than ten seconds.

BALANCING

Proper balance is very important, and the weight of the entire model must be centered on the wing, or the lift provided will be offset. Stable flight is almost impossible without proper balance, which you can adjust using either a paper clip or a small amount of tissue paper. You can make finer adjustments with the transparent tape. Cardstock models are usually light enough to be affected by the weight of small amounts of tape.

When held on two fingertips as shown in FIG. 2, models should balance with the nose slightly lower than the tail. The balance point for your fingertips should be near the middle of the wing. On some models, this might be difficult, and a few gentle test flights might by required.

If balancing the model on your fingers is not easy, a couple of test flights might help indicate where adjustments in weight are needed, if any. When flying properly balanced with the elevators straight, the model should not tend to dive steeply, nor should it nose up and stall suddenly. Gently toss the model straight and level, being careful not to twist or flip it as you launch it.

If the model noses down drastically and you have balanced the model using the detailed instructions for it, add a small amount of tape around the rear of the fuse-lage or on the rear of the fin to help balance it. A model that needs this kind of initial adjustment is uncommon.

If the model noses up and stalls severely on your test flight, it means that per-haps a little more weight is needed in the nose. This is a much more common prob-

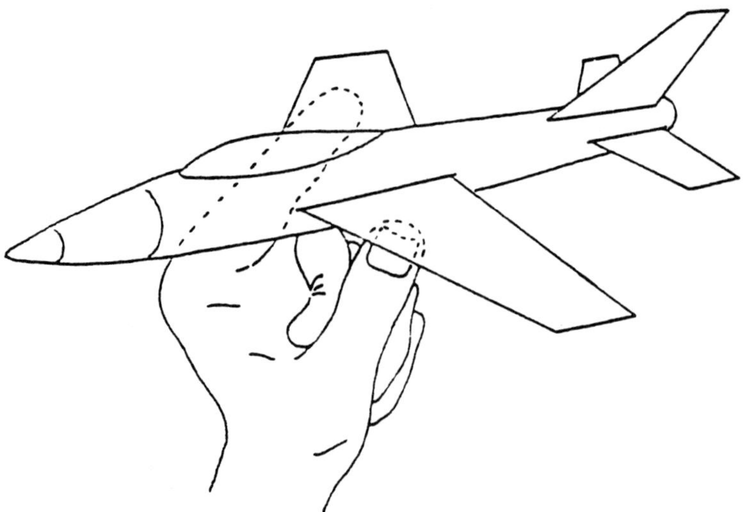

Fig. 2. To check for proper balance, hold the model on your fingertips as shown. When balanced near the center of each wing, the nose of the model should be lower than the tail. If not, add weight to the nose.

lem, because it seems that most models are a little tail heavy more often than not. Reinforcing the nose of the model might not improve the appearance, but it will help solve a tail-heavy balance problem, and the model will prove to be more rugged during hard landings.

For initial flights, grasp the model by the middle of the fuselage below the wing, as shown in FIG. 3. For models that have the wing in the way for this technique, hold the model near the nose or near the tail, whichever works best for you. Point the model in the direction of flight, hold it level, and toss it lightly into the air. Try not to twist or angle the model as you release it, and use a long sweep of your arm in a steady toss. Flinging or flipping the model is not recommended because spin and twist might be imparted, causing erratic flying. High-speed launches for greater speed and performance are explained in the section *Advanced Techniques*.

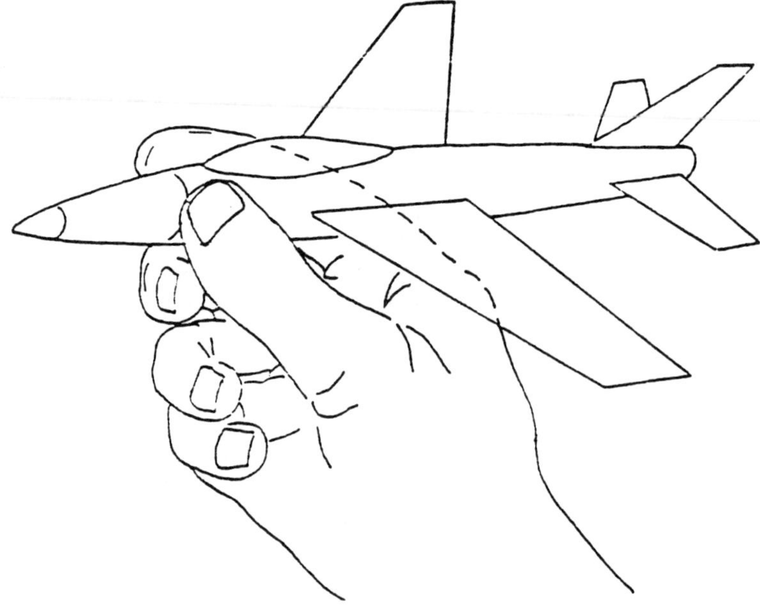

Fig. 3. A common way to grasp a model for normal flying is to hold the model near the wing. Toss gently forward and try not to flip or twist the model as you throw it. Use a smooth and level throwing form.

Control Surfaces

You usually can correct any undesired aspects of flight by adjusting the control surfaces on the wings and tail. These surfaces include the ailerons, flaps, elevators, and rudder. (See FIG. 4.) The ailerons on the wings provide roll control, and can be used to correct an improper tendency of a model to roll over in flight. Wing flaps are used to increase low-speed stability. The elevators are used to control diving or climbing. The rudder provides turning ability and can also control rolling side to side.

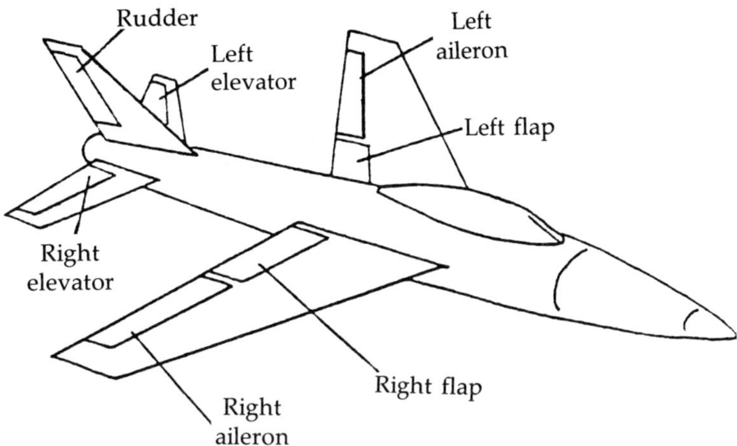

Fig. 4. All of the conventional control surfaces of a full-size aircraft, as shown in this illustration, are provided on every model glider.

To correct a model's tendency to roll or spin, bend one of the ailerons down slightly. For instance, if the model rolls to the right, bend the right-side aileron down and test-fly the model again. By bending the aileron down, that side of the wing will produce more lift and correct the roll.

To correct a tendency of the model to dive or climb steeply, first check the balance, as described previously. If the balance is correct and the model still dives too steeply, bend the rear of both of the elevator surfaces slightly upward. This will push the tail down, and help achieve level flight. Bend the elevator surfaces upward equally on both sides of the tail. Any difference in the angle of elevators will impart roll, similar to the way ailerons provide roll.

You can use the rudder at the tail of the model to control turns and rolls, but it produces less effect at high speeds. Refer to FIG. 5 showing the corrective actions for unwanted stalls, dives, and turns.

Use caution when flying models indoors. Do not fly them into other people, and avoid hitting furniture, walls, and other obstacles. In addition to the potential for becoming a nuisance, cardstock models will last much longer if they do not sustain damage from hitting things.

A basic maneuver to try after first becoming familiar with launching is the S-turn. Since rudder control has effects that vary with speed, you can achieve a change in turn direction as the model flies because it always slows down once it leaves your hand. With a model that otherwise flies straight, bend the rudder slightly to the left. When launching, try to throw the model at an angle to the right so that it turns right as you release it. When done properly, the right turn will change to a left turn during the flight. This S-turn can also be performed in the opposite direction, with right rudder and a left-turn toss. (Refer to FIG. 6.)

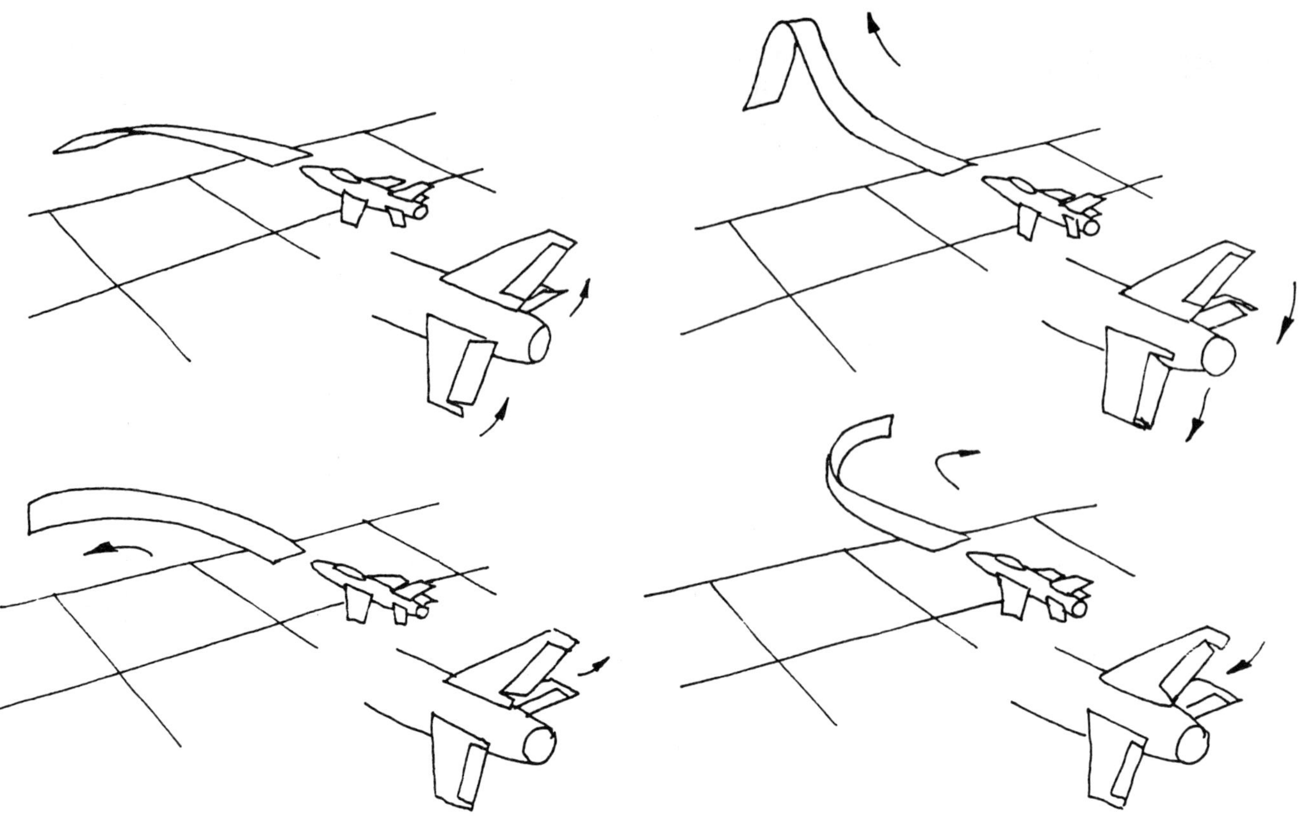

Fig. 5. Corrective actions for unwanted characteristics include bending the elevator up to correct dives, and bending it down to correct stalls. Be sure to adjust both elevators equally. To correct turns, use the rudder.

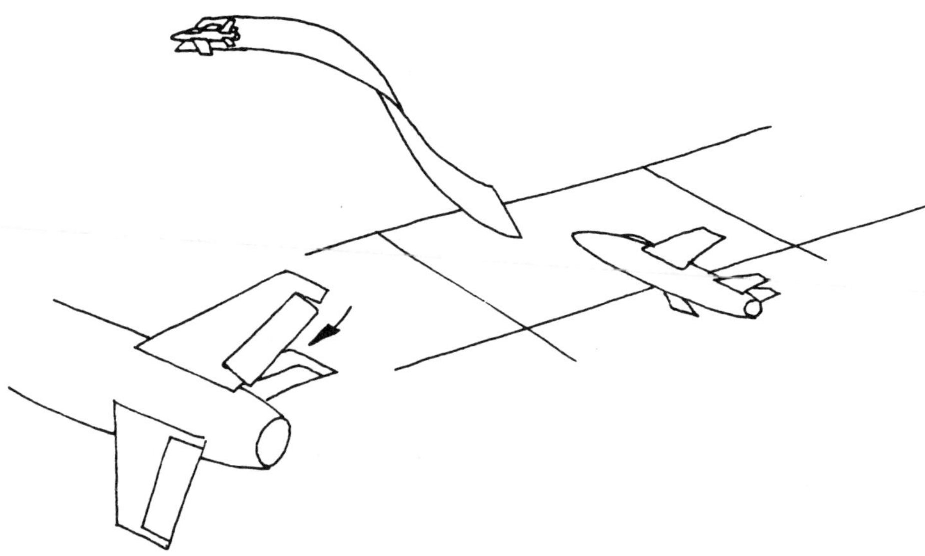

Fig. 6. For flying the standard ''S-turn'' maneuver, adjust the rudder to the left for a left-hand turn. When launching, angle the model over to the right and throw into a right-hand bank.

Stability

In normal straight-and-level flying, when a model slows down too much before landing, it will cease to produce enough lift and will 'stall'. This problem might cause the model to rock back and forth, or even to roll suddenly and spin into the ground. Wing rocking or a sudden roll during a stall usually occurs when one wingtip stalls before the other.

The cure for this problem is called *wash-out*, and involves twisting both wingtips forward slightly, as shown in FIG. 7. Even though it does result in a small loss in overall lift, this down twist keeps the wingtips from stalling before the rest of the wing. The technique is used on almost all modern jut fighters, and the minor loss of lift should not need any elevator compensation.

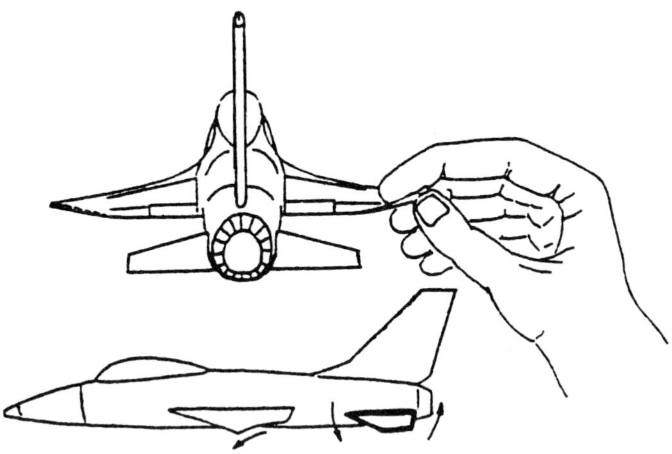

Fig. 7. To prevent spins and tip-stalling, twist the front of each wingtip downward. Also be sure the stabilizer is angled down at the front for the proper angle of incidence.

OUTDOOR FLYING

Outdoor flying makes it possible to get the greatest performance from the models, because of the benefit from any breezes or light wind. The wind can help keep the model aloft. Building the models as light as possible might not be appropriate for flying outdoors, however, because models might need to be heavier for better wind penetration. So, some models can have extra tape to reinforce and provide weight to fly best outdoors. Because of the extra weight needed for outdoor flying, you might need to build some models for indoor flying, and others just for flying outdoors. All of the models are equally suited for either type of flying.

With outdoor flying, there is sometimes the possibility of losing the models in trees, bushes, or the tops of buildings. Use care to avoid this situation, since losing a scale model airplane is often rather frustrating, and trying to retrieve models on buildings and in trees can be hazardous.

Advanced Techniques

A proven technique for getting maximum performance is known as *crossing-up* the rudder and aileron controls. For outdoor flying and fast launches, this technique involves bending an aileron down for one direction of turn and bending the rudder over for turn in the other direction. Bend the left aileron down, for instance, and bend the rudder over to the left as well. Left aileron down will cause the model to try to turn right, as described before. Bending the rudder to the left induces turns to the left, mostly at low speeds. Also add a small amount of up elevator. (See FIG. 8.)

When thrown briskly, a model with surfaces set like this will climb straight up into a half-loop, and at the top of the loop will roll over into level flight at considerable speed. It will then circle back around to the direction in which it was first launched, particularly if this was into the wind. The model will be 50 feet overhead very quickly, and circling slowly in a rather level attitude. Long flights are a direct result.

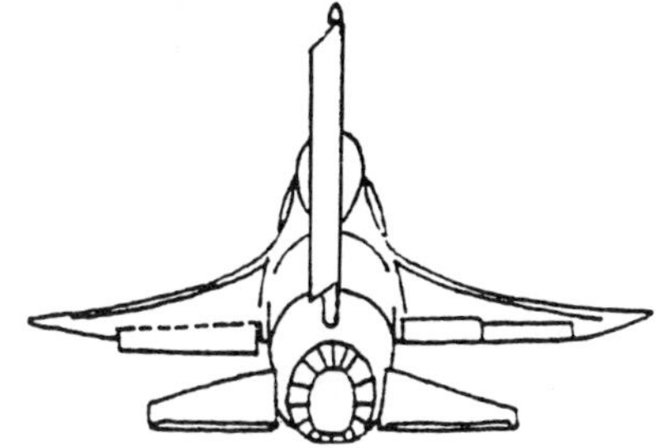

Fig. 8. The highest performance flights are possible using crossed-up controls. The left aileron causes an initial right roll, and the left rudder causes a left turn when the model slows down.

A good technique of construction which makes brisk or even very hard launches easy is a simple modification known as *finger stretch*. This is a hole or slot cut in the bottom of the plane for the thrower's finger. Position the hole just ahead of the center of the fuselage. Use the hole for your finger to propel the model during launch, instead of grasping it between the finger and thumb as shown earlier. Some models are not suited for this technique and do not have marks for it. (Refer to FIG. 9.)

The finger stretch allows you to get the most out of hand and wrist actions during launch, and the single-point 'hold' on the airplane lets the model assume the best attitude for flight before being released. This technique reduces the effect of twisting the model while throwing, and is essential for high-speed performance and long flights.

Fig. 9. Highest performance results from the very stable and fast launches made possible by a finger stretch.

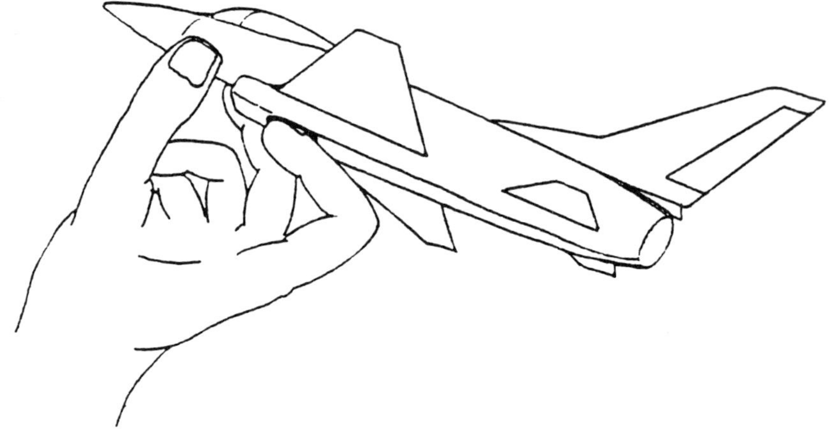

General Instructions

SPECIFIC DETAILS AND DIRECTIONS FOR COMPLETION OF EACH MODEL fighter are provided here. Read the corresponding *Detailed Instructions* when you decide to build each model. The only details contained in these brief sections are those not covered in the *General Discussion*.

You will find that each of the detailed sections follows the same steps as in the general section. No particular order is implied for building the nine models of this volume. Characteristics such as ease of building, better appearance, or better flying are simply a matter of personal preference.

The effect of improper alignment on appearance is easily noticed, and you will want to be proud of the way your model airplanes resemble the full-size aircraft. The effect of improper alignment on flying characteristics can be much more frustrating, however. Potential problems caused by improper alignment can be difficult to figure out later when you are flying the airplanes, and it takes less time to prevent them now than while flying them. Proper balance is equally important, and details of weight and balance are also provided. So try to build the models as well as you can and they will provide a lot of flying fun.

After reading the general discussion, you can select any one of the models to start with, since there is no certain sequence in which to build them. The order in which the models are listed is simply determined by the date of the first operational use of the actual aircraft.

Notice the drawings marked 'A' and 'B' for each model. Notations shown on the drawings supplement the instructions. The black arrows shown in the drawings indicate where to make folds on the parts, and the white arrows show where to make cuts, such as for wing slots.

Cut Out the Parts

Carefully cut out the wing and tail parts on sheet 'A' of the model you have selected to build first. Note the arrows indicating the cuts, tabs, and fold lines, and do not cut off any of the required tabs on the parts. On sheet 'B' cut out the parts including the fuselage, stabilizers, and canopy.

After you have cut out all of the parts for a single model, check the Parts List provided in the section of *Detailed Instructions* for that model. Be sure all of the parts needed are present. Check the same section of details for any special requirements for the model.

Score Folds on the Unprinted Side

Nearly every part of each model will include *fold lines*, where the folds are made for proper shape, except for the canopy. Once all of the parts are cut out, it's a good idea to do the folding for the required parts all at once. First, use scissors to snip along the fold lines indicated for about ⅛ inch. This will mark where the fold lines are on the unprinted side.

Next, using a ballpoint pen and a ruler or other straightedge, draw a heavy line on the underside of each part between the snips with the pen. Press down firmly with the pen in order to slightly score the fold line on the unprinted side. This is recommended to make folding the parts much easier and more exact. It is a good idea to score all parts before you start to assemble any of them.

Summary

1. Note the arrows on the drawings: black for folds, white for cuts. Cut out all of the parts. Snip along the fold lines and score on the unprinted side with a ballpoint pen and ruler. Do not cut the wing slots until later. (FIG. 10)

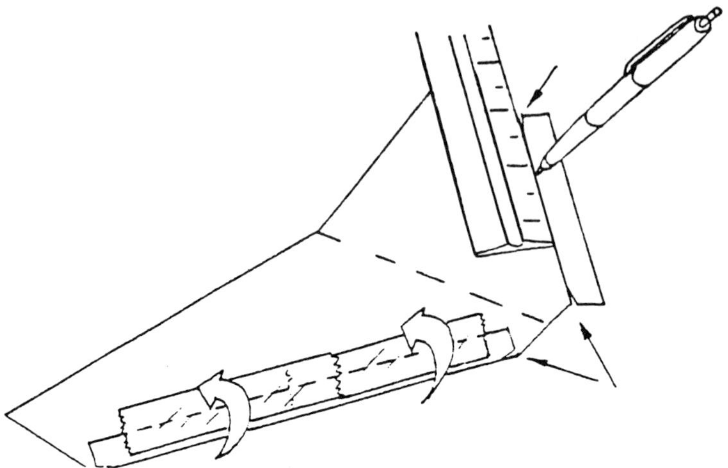

Fig. 10. Snip the fold lines as shown and score them with a ballpoint pen and a straightedge. Fold the wing tabs over and tape securely.

2. Fold the wing tabs down. Lay the wing upside down on a flat surface. Apply tape along the wing tab, fold the tab against the unprinted side of the sheet, and press down firmly. Do not warp the wing while applying tape. Repeat for all leading edges and tape them in place.
3. Form the fuselage by rolling it into a tube lengthwise. Fuselage alignment marks are used to obtain the correct shape. Align the marks. Use two short pieces of tape and 'tack' the bottom together. Check alignment, and apply plenty of tape, starting at the rear and working toward the front. (FIG. 11)

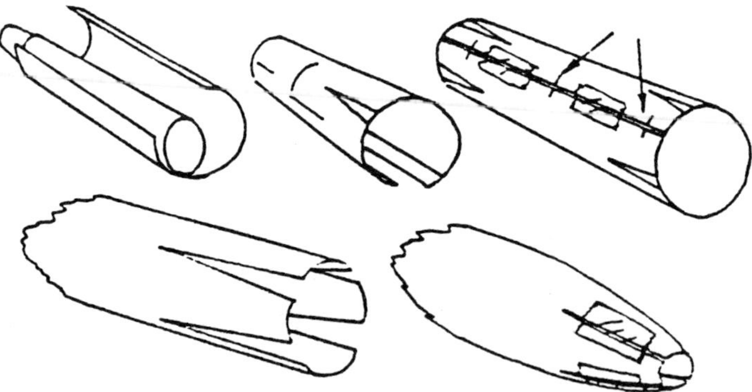

Fig. 11. Shape the fuselage by rolling it on a large pen or marker. Bring the marks on the bottom of the fuselage together and tape. After the fuselage is secured together, make the cutouts for tapering.

4. Cut the fuselage along the marks shown for tapering the front and rear. Cut out and remove the black lines of the drawing so they will not show. Apply tape and bring the tapered sections together.
5. Cut slots for the wing and stabilizer as described earlier. Insert the wing through slots in the fuselage. Align the fuselage along the lines shown on the wing. Be sure the fuselage is centered from side to side and that it is not angled to either side. Tape the wing to the fuselage sides. (FIG. 12)

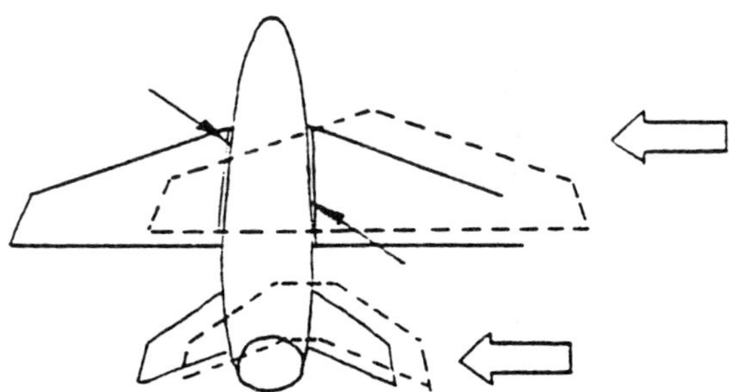

Fig. 12. Insert the wing and tail into the slots cut in the fuselage. Align the fuselage by the lines shown on the wing.

6. Leading edges of the stabilizer must be folded under as for the wing. Insert the stabilizer through the slots. Check the angle of incidence before attaching stabilizer. Secure with creased pieces of tape.

7. Fold the vertical stabilizer (tail fin) together and tape the edges. Tabs on the tail fin should extend straight out to the side. Apply tape to the tail fin tabs and position the tail fin over the rear of the fuselage. Keeping the tail fin aligned, press the tape against the fuselage sides. (FIG. 13)

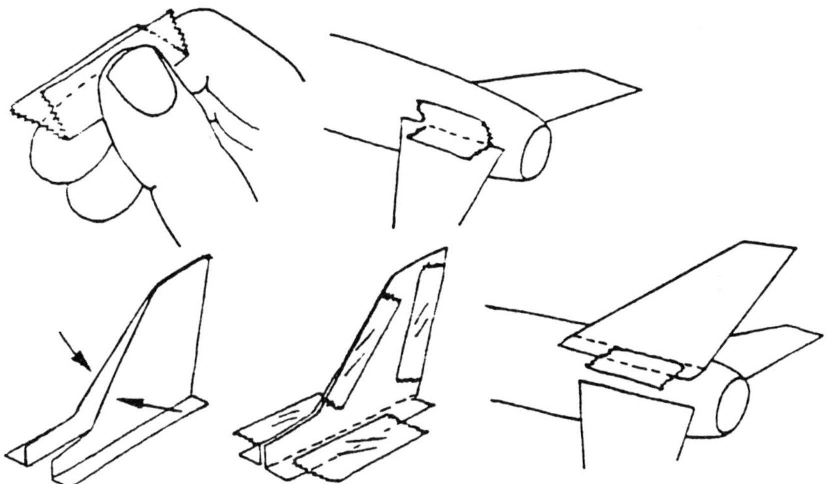

Fig. 13. Fold the vertical stabilizer (fin) together, center it on the fuselage, and tape it in place.

8. Cut off the black lines around the bottom of the canopy. Curl the canopy around a pen for a rounded shape. Bring the edges together as for the tapered parts of the fuselage. The canopy should form a ''cupped'' shape. Apply tape to the canopy and attach it onto the front of the fuselage. (FIG. 14)

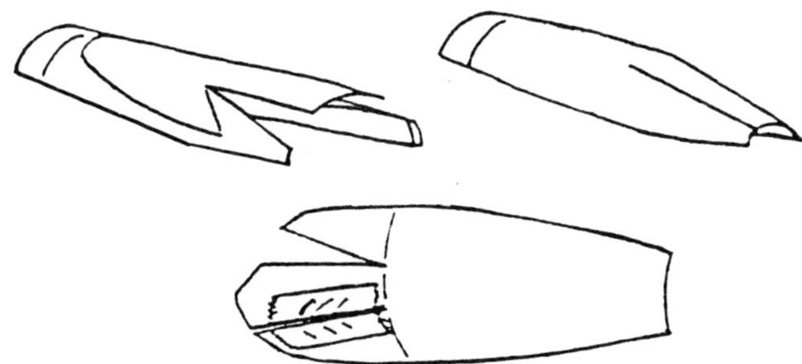

Fig. 14. Cut away the canopy outline, then curl and taper it like the fuselage. Center the canopy over the marks on the fuselage and tape it in place.

9 Using your thumbnail under the leading edge of the wing, shape a bend into the wing so that it has the proper airfoil camber. (FIG. 15)

10 Balance each model as indicated in the detailed instructions for each model. Refer to FIG. 2.

Fig. 15. With the wing upside down, use your thumbnail to shape the wing camber along the tabs on the underside of the leading edge.

Specifications & Detailed Instructions

1950 North American

F-86 Sabre

NORTH AMERICAN BEGAN A VERSION OF THIS AIRCRAFT FOR THE NAVY in 1944. After the end of World War II, captured German research indicated that the swept wing would increase performance and was incorporated into the design. As America's first great jet fighter, the F-86 won command of the skies over Korea from the Soviet-built MiG-15. Over 5000 F-86s of various types were built between 1947 and 1958, many produced under license in Canada by Canadair. The aircraft was flown by many nations, including Canada, the Netherlands, Norway, France, Italy, and Germany. Missions included air superiority, tactical bombing, and close air support.

1. Cut out all of the parts and score all fold lines.
2. Fold tabs on all parts.
3. Form the fuselage using alignment marks provided.
4. Cut away the outlines around the nose and secure all tapered areas at the front and rear.
5. Cut slots and insert the wing through the fuselage. Use creased tape and be sure the wing is aligned.
6. Check the incidence of the slots for the tail and insert it into the fuselage.
7. Assemble the vertical fin and attach it to the fuselage.
8. Cut away the outline of the canopy and fold it to shape. Align on and attach it to the fuselage.
9. Form the camber along the underside of the leading edge of the wing.
10. In addition to a standard paper clip at the bottom of the nose, the F-86 needs more weight in the nose for proper balance. Cut out a 4-×-4-inch piece of paper towel (heavy tissue) and wad it up into a ball. Insert the tissue into the opening at the rear of the model. Push the tissue all the way to the front of the model with the back of a pencil until it is positioned under the front of the canopy. The taper at the nose keeps the tissue inside.

Because of the short distance between wing and tail, the F-86 is sensitive to *pitching*, or unwanted stalls and steep dives. For this reason, it makes a good example of the benefit of *wash-out* in model form. Twist the wing tips downward, and bend the leading edge of the wing down at the tips. You can actually see the wash-out working when you are flying the model, because it helps correct severe stalls.

Table 1. Specifications for the F-86 Sabre.

TYPE	Fighter
WING SPAN	37 ft.
OVERALL LENGTH	37 ft.
GROSS WEIGHT	16,357 lbs.
CREW MEMBERS	1
PROPULSION	1 General Electric J47-GE-13 of 5200 lb. thrust
MAXIMUM SPEED	675 mph at 25,000 ft.
COMBAT RANGE	765 mi.
ARMAMENT	Six .50 cal. machine guns and four 500 lb. bombs

1955 Sukhoi

Su-7B Fitter

MAIN WING
FUSELAGE
FUSELAGE RADAR CONE
FUSELAGE NOSE SHROUD
HORIZONTAL STABILIZER
VERTICAL STABILIZER
CANOPY

The Soviet design bureau headed by Pavel Ossipovich Sukhoi produced one of its better designs just after World War II in the Su-7. Along with the supersonic interceptor version designated the Su-9, this tactical support fighter-bomber was remarkable for its time and stayed in service for many years. Although impressive for its size and power, the aircraft is known to carry only small combat loads and suffers from quite limited range.

At least 3,000 of just this first version alone were produced, and very many more of the later versions, which were more powerful and more heavily armed. These aircraft have proven to be very rugged, and are used to equip all of the Warsaw Pact nations, as well as air forces of Cuba, Egypt, Afghanistan, India, Iraq, North Korea, North Vietnam, and Syria.

1. Cut out all of the parts and score all fold lines.
2. Fold tabs on all parts.
3. Form the fuselage using the alignment marks provided.
4. Cut away the outlines around the nose and secure all tapered areas, front and rear. Curl the radar-cone pattern around and tape the edges together, forming a cone. Position the cone at the front of the fuselage and tape in place. Roll the nose shroud into a tube, and slip it over the cone and the front of the fuselage. Tape in place to complete the fuselage. (FIG. 16)
5. Cut slots and insert the wing through the fuselage. Use creased tape. Be sure the wing is aligned.
6. Check the incidence of slots for the tail and insert it into the fuselage. Tape the rear edges of the horizontal stabilizer for better strength.
7. Assemble the vertical fin and attach it to the fuselage.
8. Cut away the outline of the canopy and fold it to shape. Align on and attach it to the fuselage.
9. Form the camber along the underside of the leading edge of the wing.
10. The Su-7 is one of the easiest models to build and fly, and there are no special concerns regarding balance. Instead of a paper clip, the Su-7 needs only a 4-×-4-inch piece of tissue paper wadded up and inserted into the rear of the model, and then pushed all the way to the front with a pencil. The combination of the radar-cone type nose and the tissue paper inside make the nose of the Su-7 very rugged, and provide enough balance weight so that a paper clip is not needed at all.

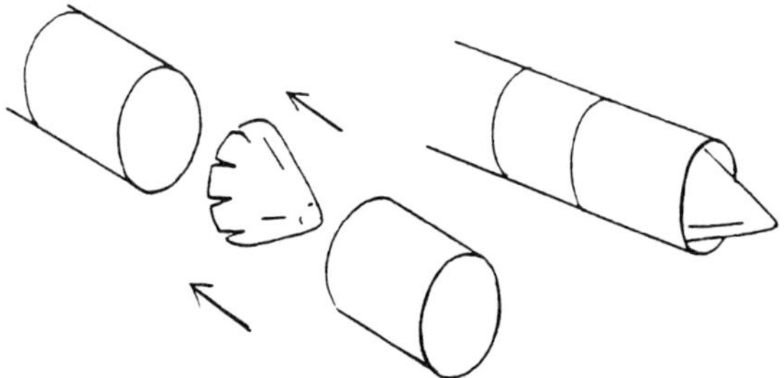

Fig. 16. Curl the radar cone and tape it together. Attach the cone to the front of the fuselage with tape. Tape the shroud together, slide it over the cone, and tape securely.

Table 3. Specifications for the Su-7.

TYPE	Fighter-Bomber
WING SPAN	29 ft.
OVERALL LENGTH	57 ft.
GROSS WEIGHT	30,200 lbs.
CREW MEMBERS	1
PROPULSION	1 Lyulka AL-7F TRD-31 of 22,000 lb. thrust
MAXIMUM SPEED	1,000 mph at 39,000 ft.
COMBAT RANGE	900 mi.
ARMAMENT	Two 30 mm cannon and 5,500 lbs. of bombs

F-100 Super Sabre

Table 6. Parts list for the F-100 Super Sabre.

MAIN WING
FUSELAGE
HORIZONTAL STABILIZER
VERTICAL STABILIZER
CANOPY

The F-100 was originally intended to perfect the F-86 design for supersonic flight. Begun in 1949, the project was accelerated because of the Korean War. Before the aircraft could become operational, however, a series of accidents led to suspension of the effort in 1954, and many design modifications were incorporated before the aircraft was finally put into service. This example is from the third production version, of which more than 1,200 were built.

With several years of peacetime service behind them, many F-100s were used during the Vietnam War, and were still being used by the United States Air National Guard into the 1970s. Known as the 'Lead Sled' because of its tendency to dive unexpectedly, the F-100 had both undesirable and redeeming qualities, including long operational life when compared to other designs of the same period.

1. Cut out all of the parts and score all fold lines.
2. Fold tabs on all parts.
3. Form the fuselage using the alignment marks provided.
4. Cut away the outlines around the nose and secure all tapered areas, at the front and rear.
5. Cut slots and insert the wing through the fuselage. Use creased tape. Be sure the wing is aligned.
6. Check the incidence of slots for the tail and insert it into the fuselage.
7. Assemble the vertical fin and attach to the fuselage.
8. Cut away the outline of the canopy and fold it to shape. Align on and attach it to the fuselage.
9. Form the camber along the underside of the leading edge of the wing.
10. The F-100 is very neat and simple in model form, and there are no surprises involved in flying it. Usually, just slipping a common paper clip onto the bottom of the nose is all that is required, but a patch of tissue wadded up inside can also be used for balance. (Refer to the details of the F-86.) Using tissue instead of a paper clip might look better, and also helps the fuselage retain its shape.

Table 5. Specifications for the F-100 Super Sabre.

TYPE	Fighter-Bomber
WING SPAN	38 ft.
OVERALL LENGTH	47 ft.
GROSS WEIGHT	34,832 lbs.
CREW MEMBERS	1
PROPULSION	1 Pratt & Whitney J57-P-21A of 17,000 lb. thrust
MAXIMUM SPEED	864 mph at 35,000 ft.
COMBAT RANGE	1,500 mi.
ARMAMENT	Four 20 mm cannon and 7,500 lbs. of bombs

1958 Mikoyan-Gurevich

MiG-21F Fishbed

*Table 8. Parts list
for the MiG-21.*

MAIN WING
FUSELAGE
FUSELAGE RADAR CONE
FUSELAGE NOSE SHROUD
HORIZONTAL STABILIZER
VERTICAL STABILIZER
CANOPY

After the series of designs during the late 1940s and early 1950s, the success of the MiG family of fighters was continued with this very popular design. Efforts began in 1954 to produce a lightweight aircraft capable of flight at twice the speed of sound. The result is an aircraft which is quite maneuverable and is a small target, but which carries a limited amount of weaponry or other load. The aircraft's range is also very limited.

Still used as a frontline fighter into the 1970s, more than 4,000 were built in the USSR, and many more were produced in Czechoslovakia, the People's Republic of China, and India. Used by more than 20 different nations, the MiG-21 is known for high performance and dogfight agility, with enjoyable flying qualities. It is also known for reliability, but with such limited weaponry and primitive radar and avionics, modern fighters like the F-15 have shot them down in ratios of more than 50 to 1.

1. Cut out all the parts and score all fold lines.
2. Fold tabs on all parts.
3. Form the fuselage using the alignment marks provided.
4. Cut away the outlines around the nose and secure all tapered areas, front and rear. Curl the radar-cone pattern around and tape the edges together, forming a cone. Position it at the front of the fuselage and tape in place. Roll the nose shroud into a tube, and slip it over the cone and the front of the fuselage. Tape in place to complete the fuselage. (Refer to FIG. 16.)
5. Cut slots and insert the wing through the fuselage. Use creased tape. Be sure the wing is aligned.
6. Check the incidence of slots for the tail and insert it into the fuselage. Tape the rear edges of the horizontal stabilizer for better strength.
7. Assemble the vertical fin and attach it to the fuselage.
8. Cut away the outline of the canopy and fold it to shape. Align on and attach it to the fuselage.
9. Form the camber along the underside of the leading edge of the wing.
10. Because it is one of the smallest models, take care that the MiG-21 does not become too heavy. Too much tape can increase the weight of this model very quickly. Insert a patch of heavy tissue paper into the tail of the MiG-21, as in the Su-7. Push the tissue paper all the way to the front with a long pencil. With the radar-cone type nose and the tissue balance weight, the nose area will be the proper weight, and also be very strong.

Table 7. Specifications for the MiG-21.

TYPE	Fighter
WING SPAN	23 ft.
OVERALL LENGTH	45 ft.
GROSS WEIGHT	16,700 lbs.
CREW MEMBERS	1
PROPULSION	1 Tumanskii R-11 turbojet/AB, 12,676 lb. thrust
MAXIMUM SPEED	1,243 mph at 35,000 ft.
COMBAT RANGE	375 mi.
ARMAMENT	One 30 mm cannon and 2 K-13 air-to-air missiles

F-105D Thunderchief

Table 10. Parts list for the F-105.

MAIN WING
FUSELAGE
RIGHT AIR INTAKE
LEFT AIR INTAKE
HORIZONTAL STABILIZER
VERTICAL STABILIZER
CANOPY

At the close of a decade of steady advancement, Republic developed a new and much more capable aircraft to replace the early F-84. In 1954, the F-105 design impressed Air Force officials for its great potential, and this was successfully realized when production of the aircraft started less than three years later. This 'D' version was the principal production version, of which 600 were built and put into service.

In addition to the characteristics of versatility and formidable weaponry, the F-105 exhibited very good performance at twice the speed of sound. Known affectionately as 'Thud,' the aircraft was used extensively as a fighter-bomber in the Vietnam War. During the period of 1963 to 1968, F-105s carried out over 75 percent of bombing missions flown by the Air Force.

1. Cut out all of the parts and score all fold lines.
2. Fold tabs on all parts.
3. Form the fuselage using the alignment marks provided.
4. Cut away the outlines around the nose and secure all tapered areas, at the front and rear.
5. Cut slots and insert the wing through the fuselage. Use creased tape. Be sure the wing is aligned. Note the lateral air intakes and their positioning. Refer to FIG. 17 for the positioning of this type of air intake.
6. Check the incidence of the tail slots and insert the stabilizer into the slots.
7. Assemble the vertical fin and attach it to the fuselage.
8. Cut away the outline of the canopy and fold it to shape. Align on and attach it to the fuselage.
9. Form the camber along the underside of the leading edge of the wing.
10. As one of the easiest to build and fly, the F-105 is recommended if you have never built a complex paper airplane. It has excellent stability as a result of its rather large size, and has proven to be very rugged. Balance by using a 4-×-4-inch piece of tissue paper in a wad and inserted into the tail cone. Push the tissue all the way to the front with a pencil. If the model still seems too tail heavy, add a second patch of tissue. Normally, a paper clip is not needed, and the tissue paper helps the large fuselage retain its shape.

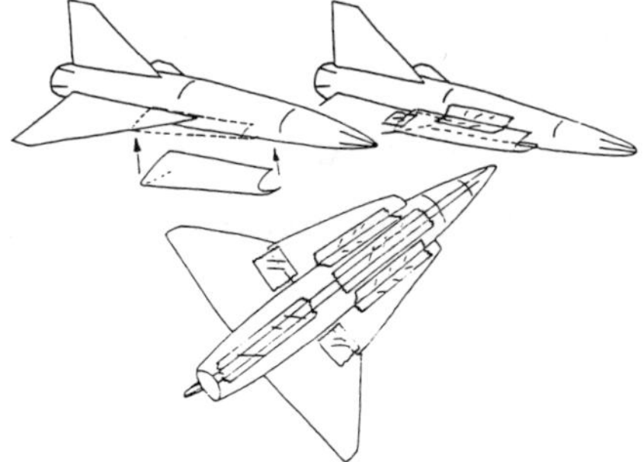

Fig. 17. Curl the air intake parts into a half-round shape and position each next to the fuselage. Tape the rear of the intake to the wing first, and then to the fuselage sides.

Table 9. Specifications for the F-105.

TYPE	Fighter-Bomber
WING SPAN	34 ft.
OVERALL LENGTH	64 ft.
GROSS WEIGHT	52,984 lbs.
CREW MEMBERS	1
PROPULSION	1 Pratt & Whitney J57-P-19W of 26,500 lb. thrust
MAXIMUM SPEED	1,390 mph at 356,000 ft.
COMBAT RANGE	1,840 mi.
ARMAMENT	One 20 mm 6-bbl. cannon, 14,000 lbs. of bombs

1959 Avions Marcel Dassault
Etendard IV-M

MAIN WING
FUSELAGE LEFT FRONT
FUSELAGE RIGHT FRONT
FUSELAGE LEFT REAR
FUSELAGE RIGHT REAR
HORIZONTAL STABILIZER
VERTICAL STABILIZER
CANOPY

Maintaining their leadership of French aviation, the Dassault designers produced this quite useful carrier-borne fighter and first flew it in 1956. The Etendard was the first supersonic jet fighter produced in Europe able to be flown from an aircraft carrier at sea. As a very conventional design, the Etendard was a departure from the delta-wing design of so many other French combat aircraft. This has provided better versatility, and although few have been built, the total production also included a version intended for photoreconnaissance.

A redesign and upgrade during the 1970s resulted in the more powerful and sophisticated Super Etendard. This aircraft proved itself in combat when it was being operated by Argentine Air Forces, and a Super Etendard using a French Exocet missile is credited with the destruction of the British destroyer H.M.S. *Sheffield*. Even though this later version retains its carrier operation capability, there are no countries flying the Etendard that have aircraft carriers.

1. Cut out all of the parts and score all fold lines.
2. Fold tabs on all parts.
3. Form the fuselage using the alignment marks provided. Attach the fuselage at the bottom first, then along the top. Tape all of the parts securely. Use care when cutting around the details of the lateral air intakes. (FIG. 18)
4. Cut away the outlines around the nose and secure all tapered areas, front and rear. Assemble the nose section and overlap it onto the rear. Tape securely, on both the top and bottom. (Fig. 19)
5. Cut slots and insert the wing through the fuselage. Use creased tape. Be sure the wing is aligned.
6. Check the incidence of slots for the tail and insert the stabilizer into vertical fin. Use creased pieces of tape to secure the stabilizer to the fin. (FIG. 20)
7. Assemble the vertical fin and attach it to the fuselage.
8. Cut away the outline of the canopy and fold it to shape. Align on and attach it to the fuselage.
9. Form the camber along the underside the leading edge of the wing.
10. When the tail configuration is properly assembled, these models have demonstrated excellent stability. A paper clip might not be needed if you use a patch of tissue for balance. Insert a tissue wad into the rear of the model and push it all the way to the front with a pencil. Any problems with flying the Etendard may be traced to the angle of incidence of the stabilizer.

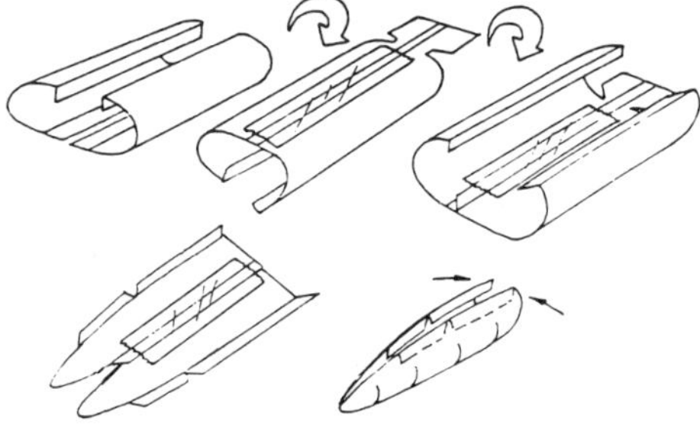

Fig. 18. Assemble the bottom of the four-piece fuselage first, including the inside of the overlap. The nose section is also started at the bottom.

Table 11. Specifications for the Etendard.

TYPE	Fighter
WING SPAN	31 ft.
OVERALL LENGTH	47 ft.
GROSS WEIGHT	22,486 lbs.
CREW MEMBERS	1
PROPULSION	1 SNECMA Atar 8 turbojet of 9,700 lb. thrust
MAXIMUM SPEED	683 mph at sea level
COMBAT RANGE	765 mi.
ARMAMENT	Two 30 mm cannon and 3,000 lbs. of bombs

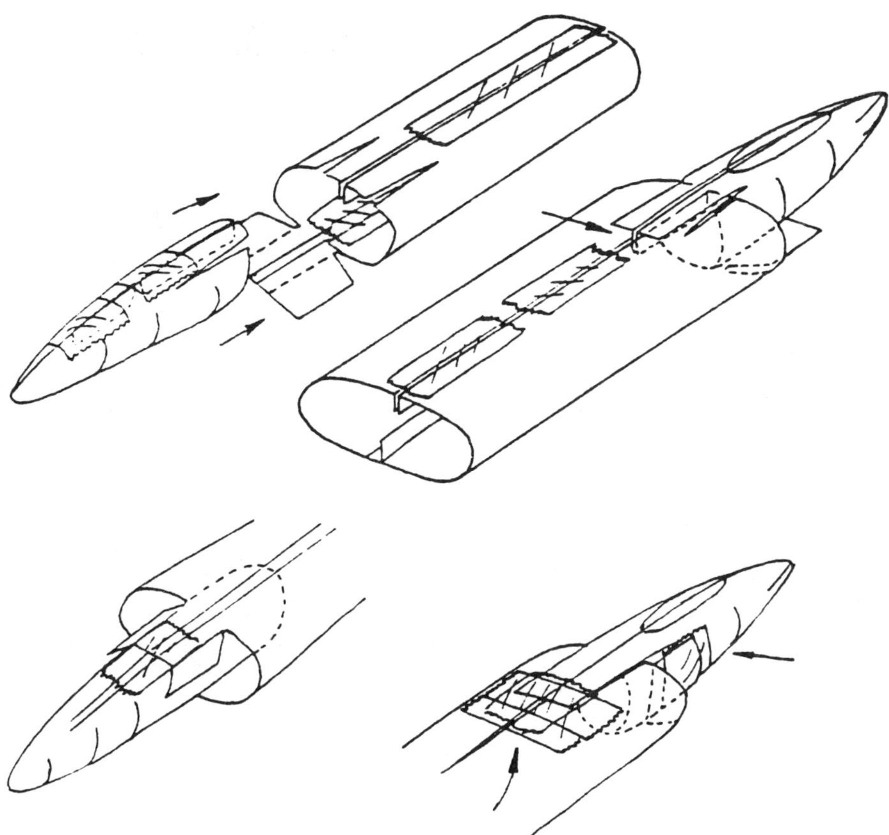

Fig. 19. The top of the fuselage forms a ''T-beam'' and uses a butt joint for strength. The T-beam of the front should be inserted between the tabs of the T-beam area of the rear. Apply tape to the top, bottom, and sides.

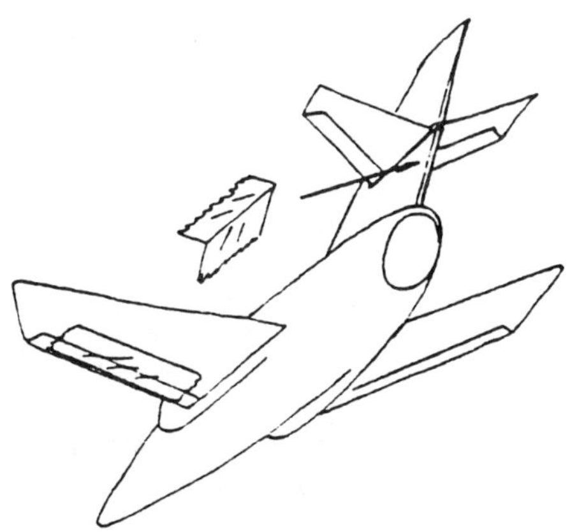

Fig. 20. The Etendard has a ''semi T-tail'' with the stabilizer inserted into the slot cut for it halfway up the vertical fin. Use creased pieces of tape.

F-4B Phantom II

Table 14. Parts list for the F-4 Phantom.

MAIN WING
FUSELAGE LEFT FRONT
FUSELAGE RIGHT FRONT
FUSELAGE LEFT REAR
FUSELAGE RIGHT REAR
EXHAUST CENTER SHROUD
HORIZONTAL STABILIZER
VERTICAL STABILIZER
CANOPY

Considered the best fighter-bomber ever built, this versatile and powerful aircraft is in a class by itself in that more than 5,000 have been produced and put into service. First flown in 1958, the design requirements from the Navy were for an all-weather attack fighter which had to fly faster than the speed of sound. Changes in the operational needs during development caused additional delays, but the result has proved very worthwhile. Great potential was also seen by the Air Force early on, and McDonnell-Douglas was asked to make an improved version.

The F-4 was in continued production for twenty years, with the 5,000th aircraft built on the 24th of May 1978. Many different versions were produced for the Navy, the Air Force, and the Marines, and hundreds are operated by other nations, including Great Britain, Germany, Iran, Israel, Spain, Japan, Greece, and Turkey. The F-4 is known for the powerful performance made possible by the twin J79 afterburning engines, and all versions carry a large radar, formidable weaponry, and large fuel capacity. During the Vietnam War, Air Force and Navy F-4 Phantoms accomplished air supremacy and flew thousands of tactical bombing missions.

1. Cut out all of the parts and score all fold lines.
2. Fold tabs on all parts.
3. Form the squared fuselage using the alignment marks provided. Tape the fuselage at the bottom first, then along the top. Tape all parts securely. Use care when cutting around details at the lateral air intakes. Refer to FIG. 19 for the steps in assembling this type of fuselage.
4. Cut away the outlines around the nose and secure all tapered areas, at the front and rear. Assemble the nose section and overlap it onto the rear. Tape the parts securely, on both the top and bottom.
5. Cut slots and insert the wing through the fuselage. Use creased tape. Be sure the wing is aligned.
6. Refer to FIG. 21 for the illustration of the tail of the F-4 Phantom. This design is both accurate in scale appearance and is very strong, without being too heavy. It is somewhat complex to assemble, but the proper angle of incidence of the tail is very easy to achieve.
7. Assemble the vertical fin and tape it to the fuselage.
8. Cut away the outline of the canopy and fold to shape. Align on and attach to the fuselage.
9. Form the camber along the underside of the leading edge of the wing.
10. Using tissue to balance the F-4 is a little more difficult than with the other models, and several smaller patches of tissue might be needed in order to fit them through the exhaust cones at the rear of the model. Push the tissue all the way to the front of the nose and check for proper balance. If the Phantom stalls repeatedly during test flying, you might need to modify the air intakes. Snip the upper outside corner of each air intake, and adjust the top of the air intake so that it angles downward. On the models with large lateral intakes like the Phantom, the intakes cause severe stalling if not angled downward and taped.

TYPE	Fighter-Bomber
WING SPAN	38 ft.
OVERALL LENGTH	58 ft.
GROSS WEIGHT	54,600 lbs.
CREW MEMBERS	2
PROPULSION	2 General Electric J79-GE-8, 16,000 lb. each
MAXIMUM SPEED	1,390 mph at 36,000 ft.
COMBAT RANGE	1,840 mi.
ARMAMENT	One 20 mm 6-bbl. cannon, 14,000 lbs. of bombs

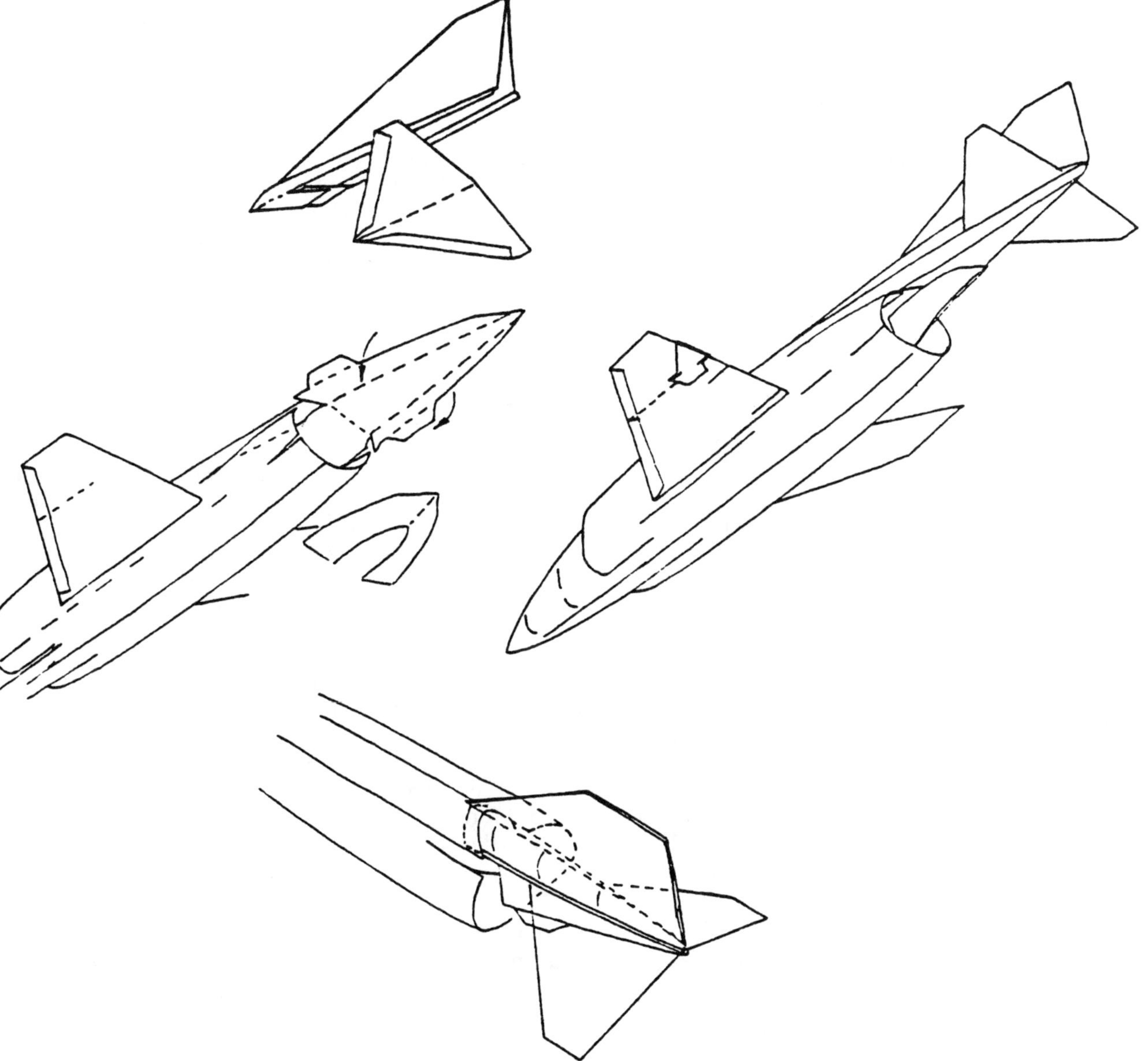

Fig. 21. Fold the sides of the tail section down and in as shown at the arrows. The stabilizer is attached in between the bottom of the fin and the top of the fuselage. The additional piece shown completes the area between the exhaust nozzles.

1962 McDonnell-Douglas
A-4E Skyhawk

The U.S. Navy began operating one of the most useful and versatile aircraft to ever serve when Douglas Aircraft started deliveries of the first A-4 Skyhawks in 1962. After convincing the Navy that the Skyhawk would fulfill expectations, Douglas chief designer Ed Heinemann produced an aircraft that weighed less than half of what the Navy had expected and immediately set new speed records. In addition to many innovations that make it light and simple, the aircraft carries both a large fuel supply and large weapon load. Also, the manufacturer maintains an active upgrade program, providing advancements in engines and avionics and extending the aircraft's 25-year history.

Over 2,900 of these aircraft have been built, including the equally successful two-seat version. Having served during the Vietnam War for the Navy, the Skyhawk is still flown by the U.S. Marine Corps and the U.S. Naval Air Advanced Training Command. Many have been exported to other countries, including Argentina, Australia, Kuwait, New Zealand, Singapore, and particularly Israel. Maintaining their own extensive update program, Israel has developed effective avionics and airframe advancements. The A-4 Skyhawks was also the aircraft used by the U.S. Navy Blue Angels Air Demonstration Team, until recent replacement with the F/A-18 Hornet.

1. Cut out all of the parts and score all fold lines.
2. Fold tabs on all parts.
3. Form the fuselage using the alignment marks provided. Attach the fuselage at the bottom first, then along the top. Tape all parts securely. Use care when cutting around details at the lateral air intakes. Refer to FIG. 19 for assembling this type of fuselage.
4. Cut away the outlines around the nose and secure all tapered areas, front and rear. Assemble the nose section and overlap it onto the rear. Tape the nose securely, on both the top and bottom.
5. Cut slots and insert the wing through the fuselage. Use creased tape. Be sure the wing is aligned.
6. Check the incidence of slots for the tail and insert the stabilizer into the vertical fin. Use creased pieces of tape to attach it to the vertical fin. Refer to FIG. 20 for the positioning of the horizontal stabilizer.
7. Assemble the vertical fin and tape it to the fuselage.
8. Cut away the outline of the canopy and fold it to shape. Align on and attach it to the fuselage.
9. Form the camber along the underside of the leading edge of the wing.
10. Even though it is just about the smallest model of the series, the A-4 Skyhawk has proven very stable and fun to fly. Balance with a patch of tissue pushed all the way from the tail cone to the nose. No paper clip should be needed. The tissue also helps strengthen the nose.

Table 15. Specifications for the A-4 Skyhawk.

TYPE	Naval Attack
WING SPAN	27 ft.
OVERALL LENGTH	40 ft.
GROSS WEIGHT	24,500 lbs.
CREW MEMBERS	1
PROPULSION	1 Pratt & Whitney J52-P-6 with 8,500 lb. thrust
MAXIMUM SPEED	685 mph at sea level
COMBAT RANGE	920 mi.
ARMAMENT	Two 20 mm cannons and 8,200 lbs. bombs

F-86 Sabre

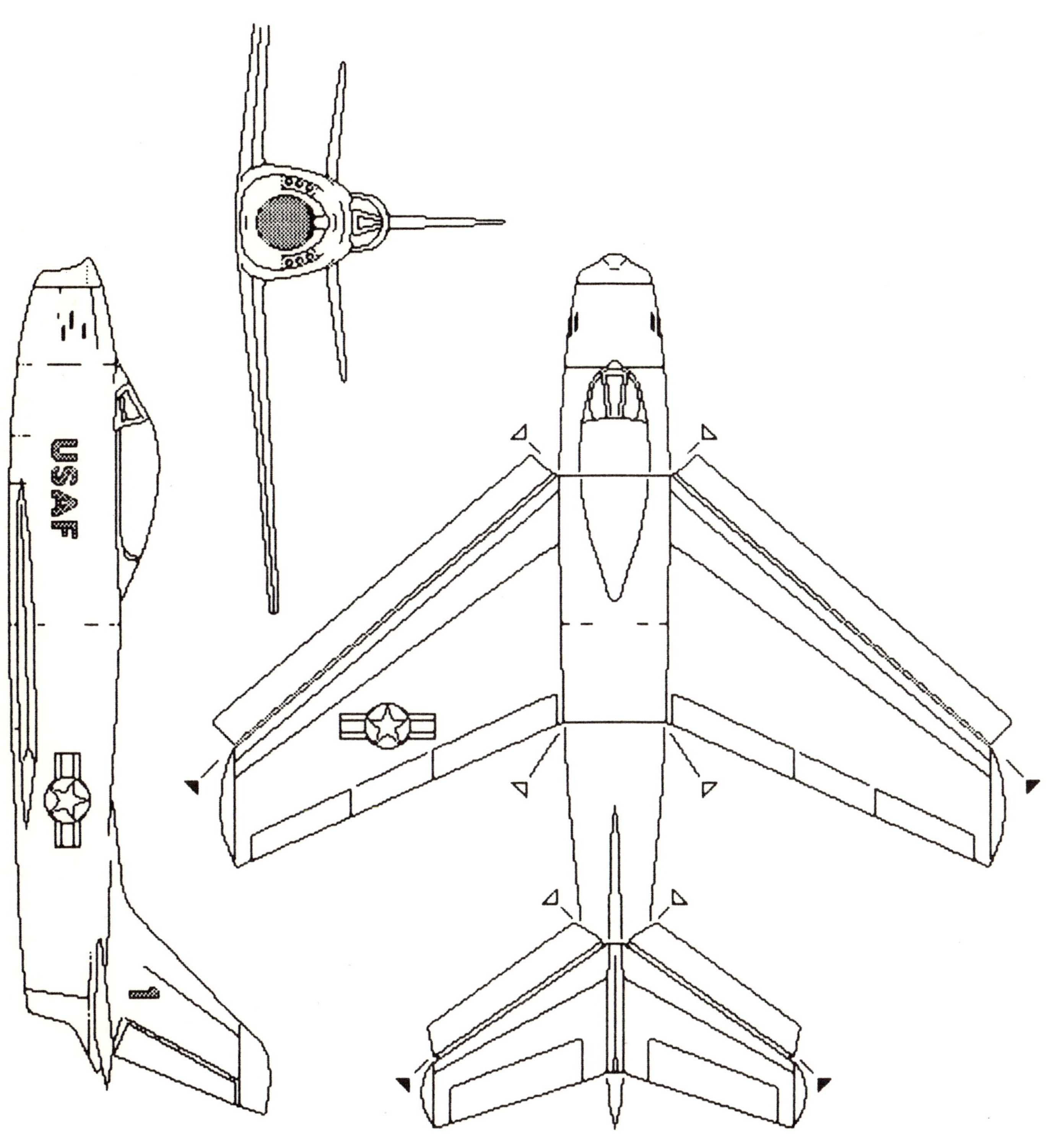

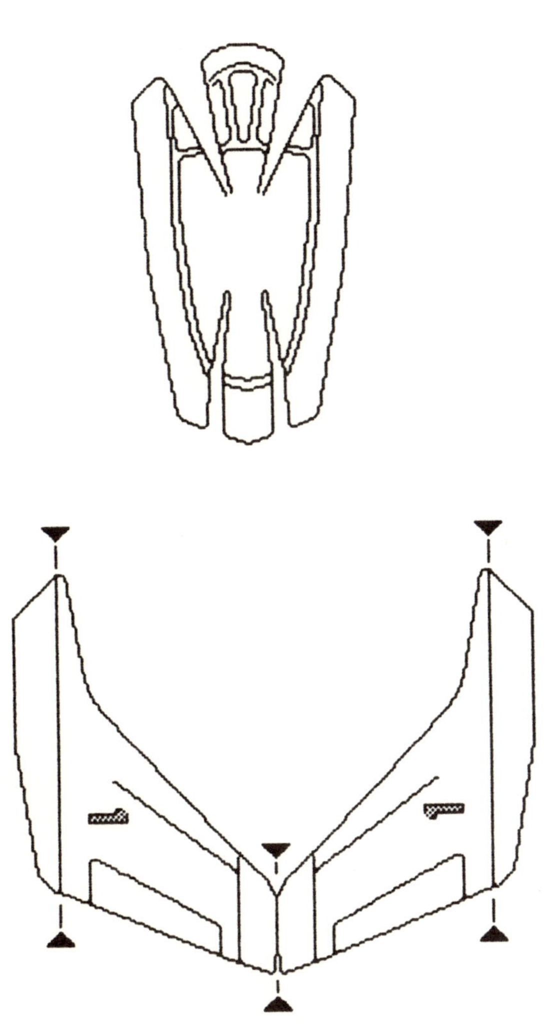
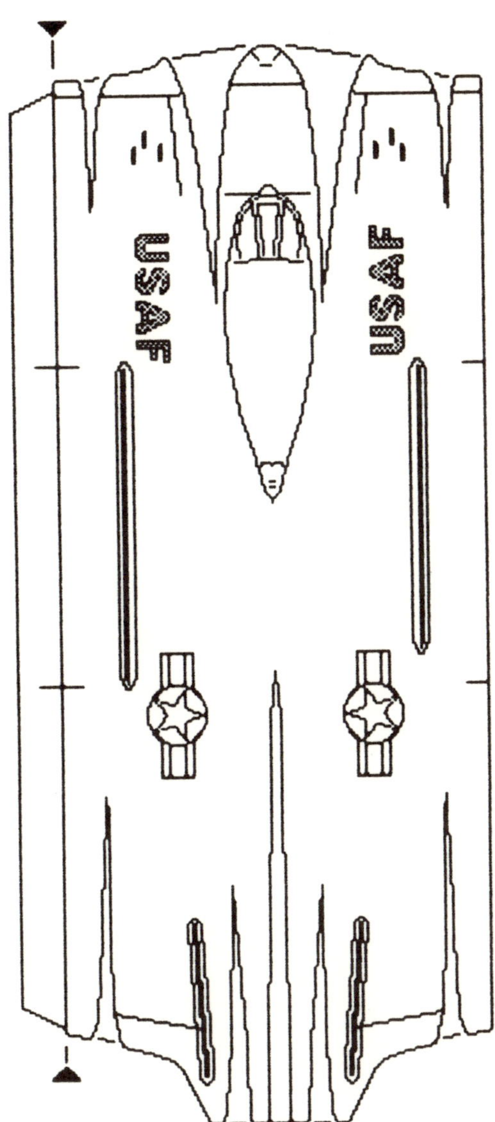

USAF
USAF

Su-7B NATO 'Fitter'

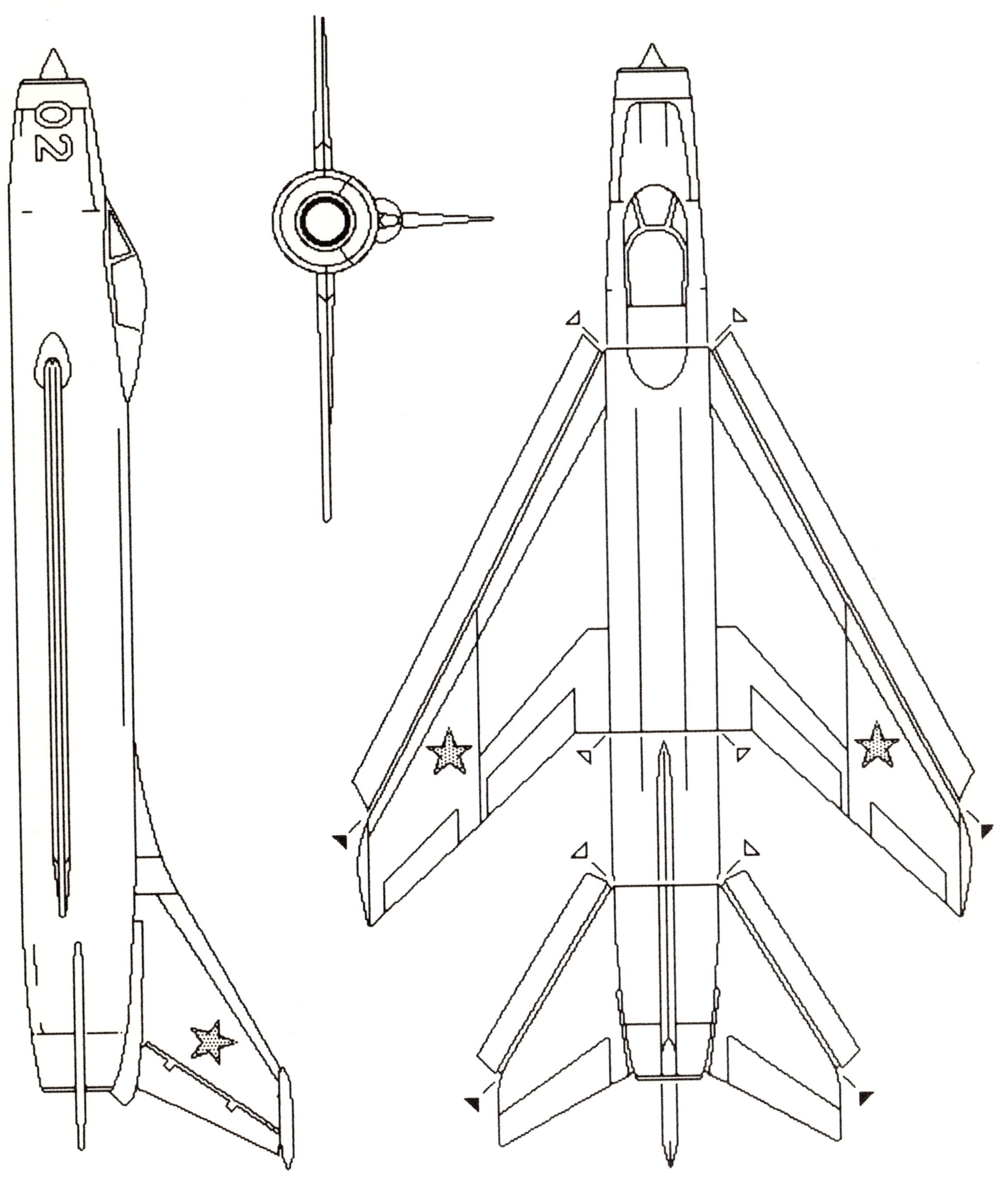

Su-7B NATO 'Fitter'

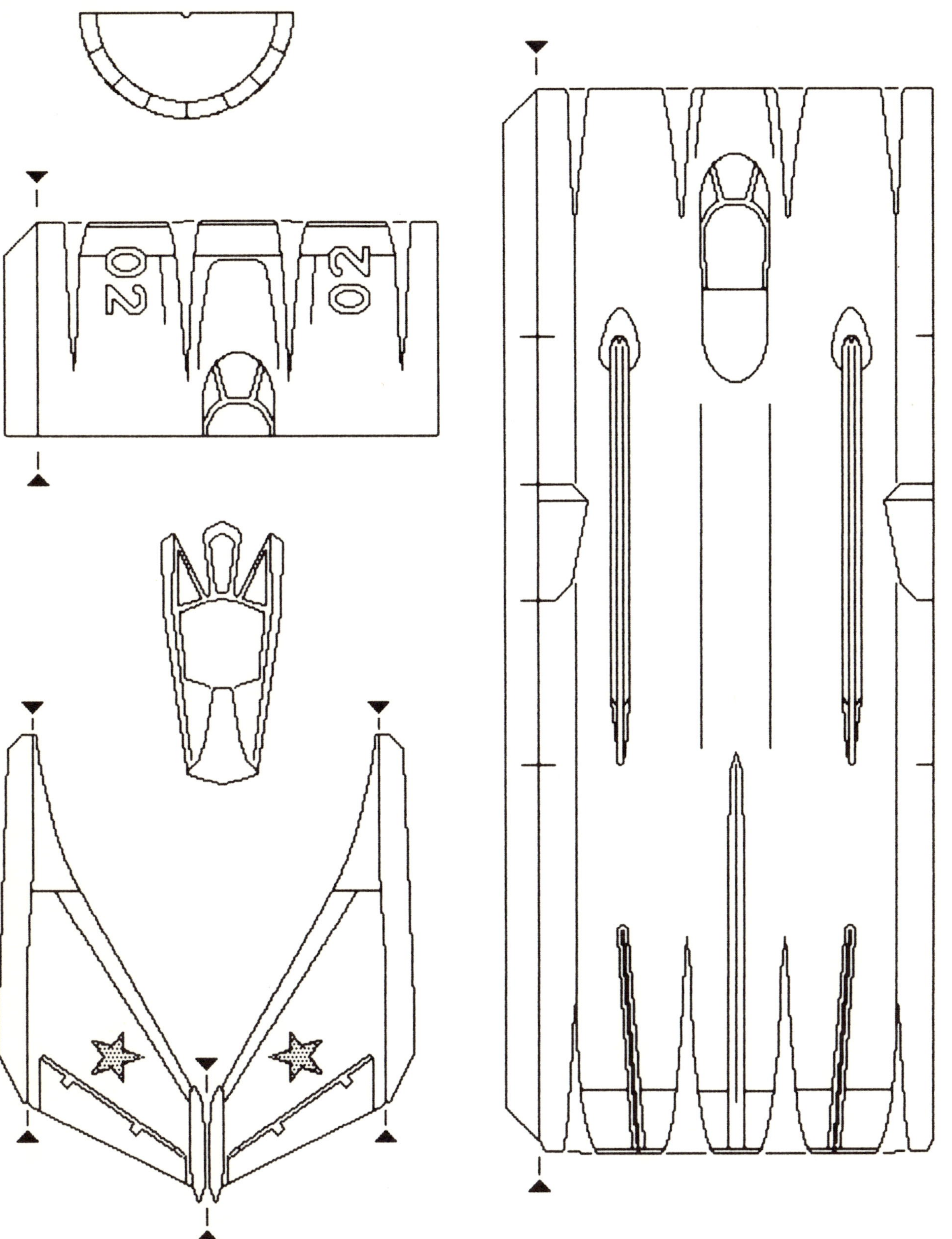

F-100 Super Sabre

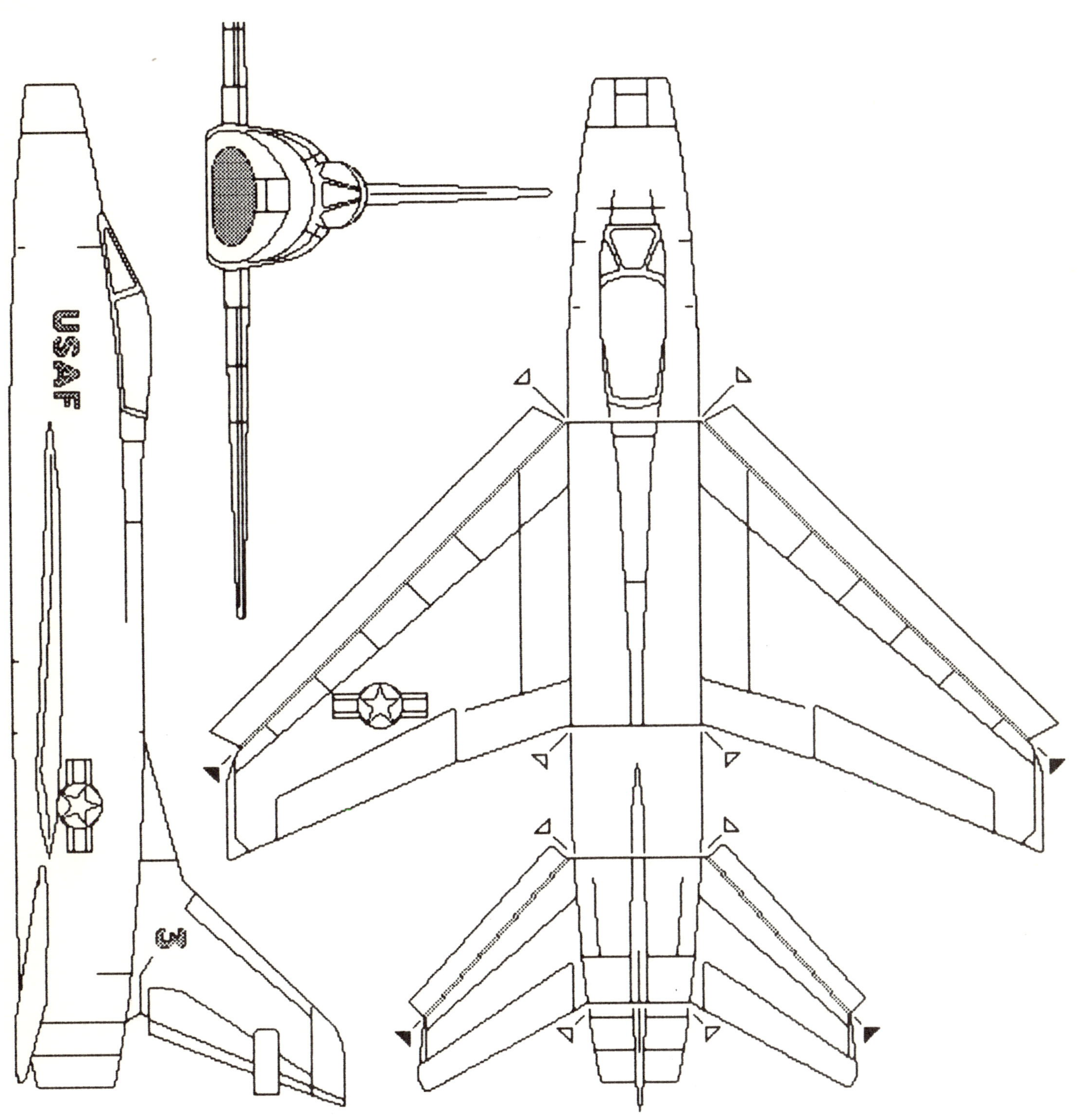

F-100 Super Sabre

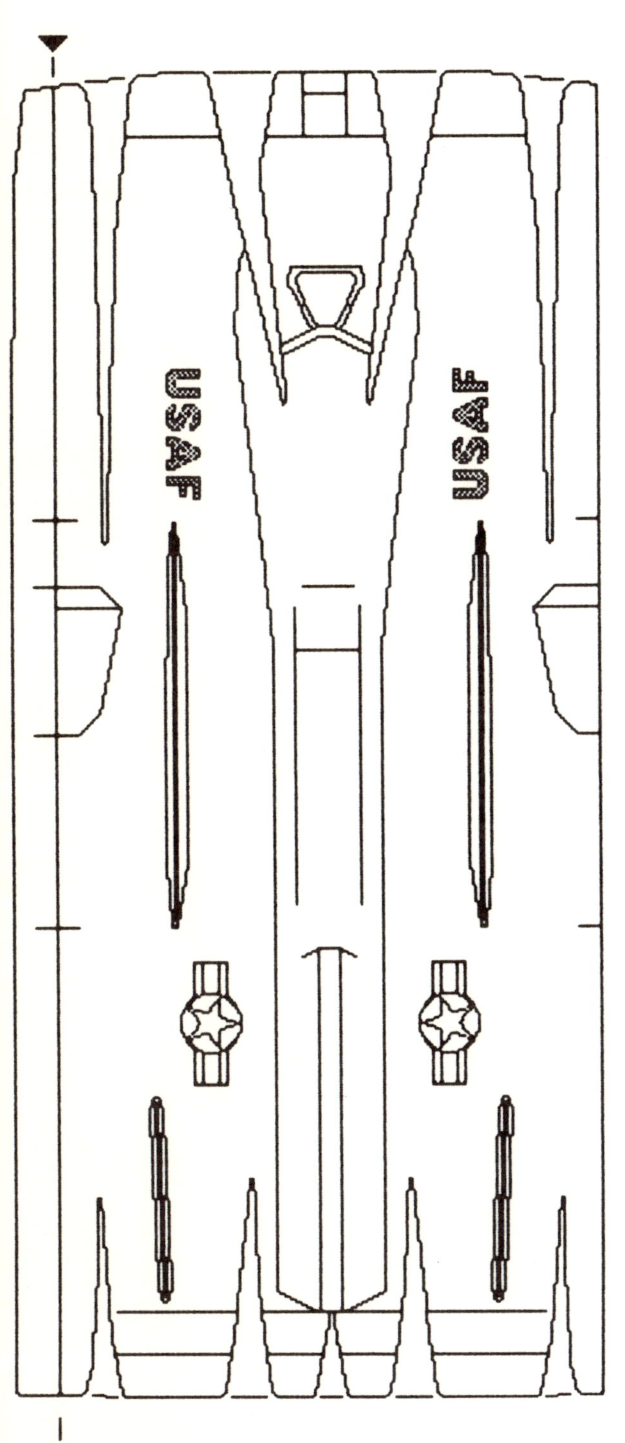

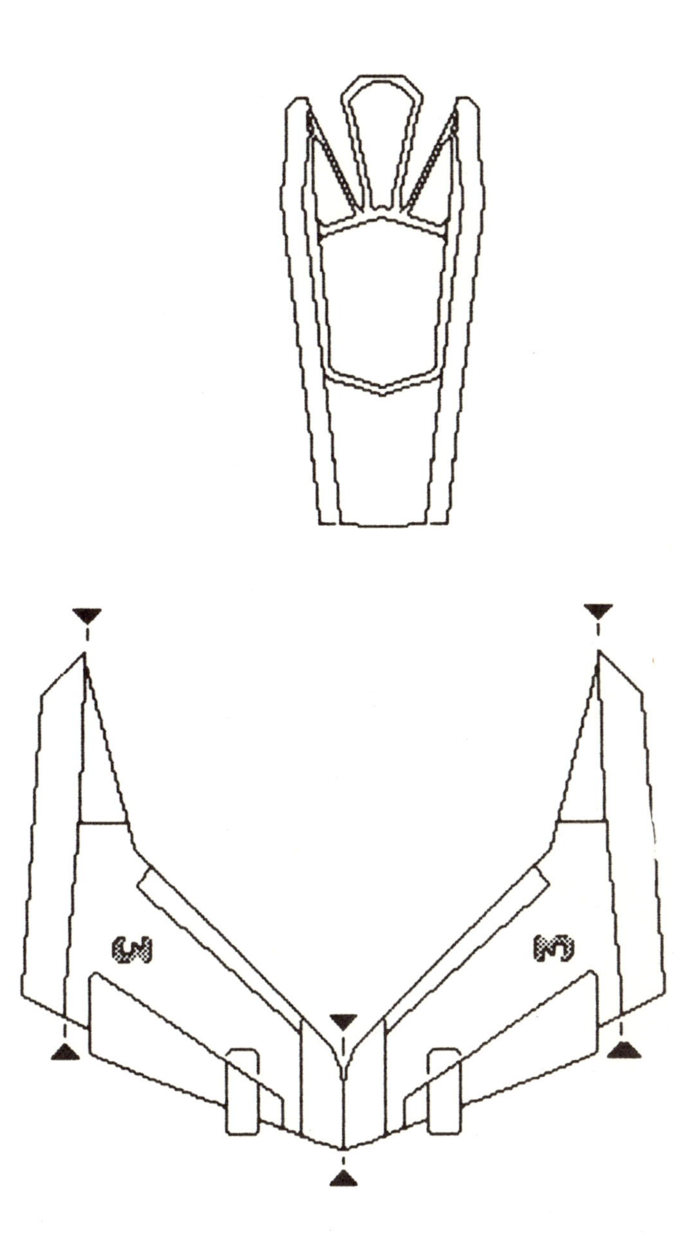

MiG-21F NATO 'Fishbed'

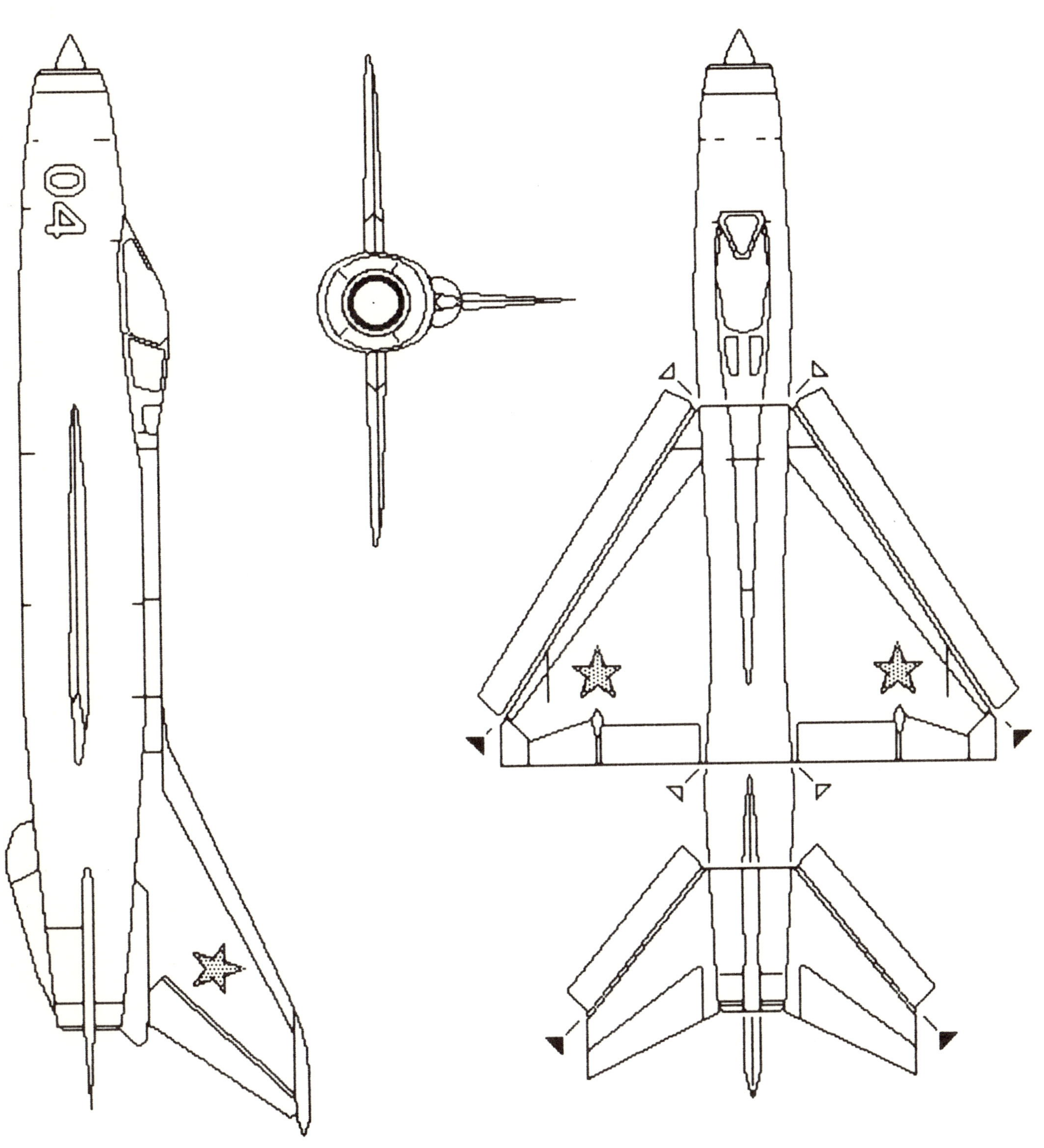

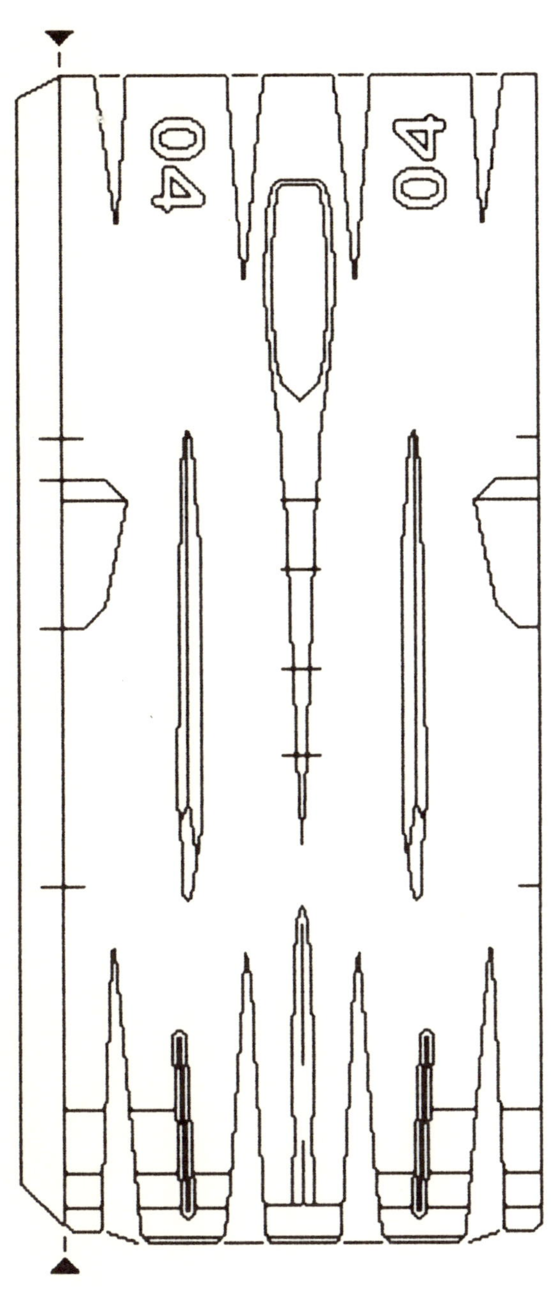

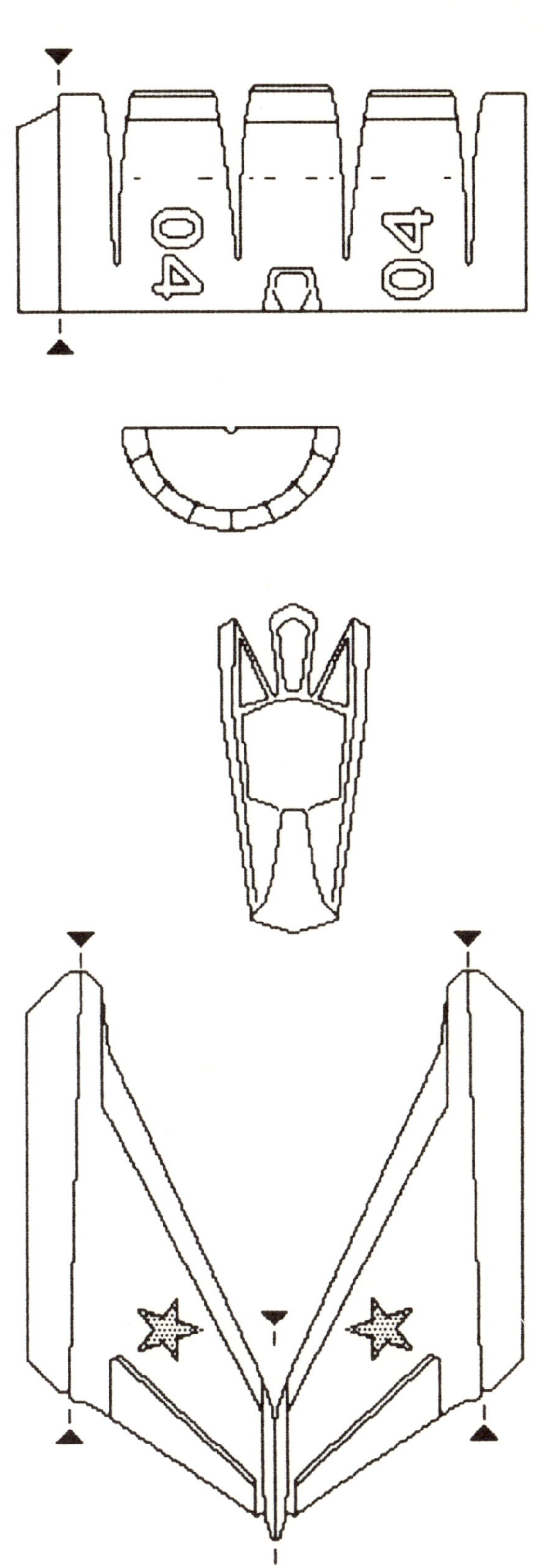

F-105 Thunderchief

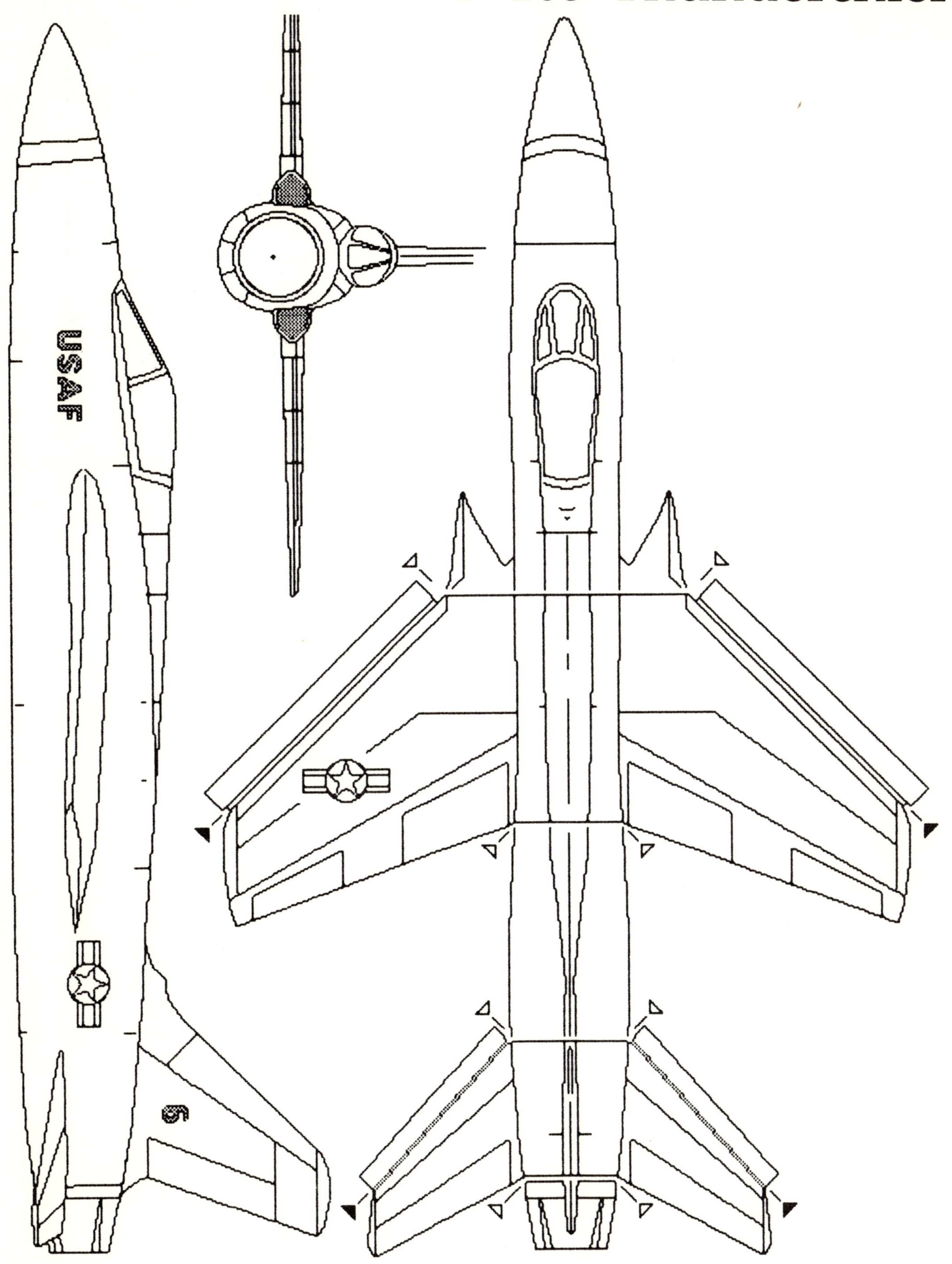

F-105 Thunderchief

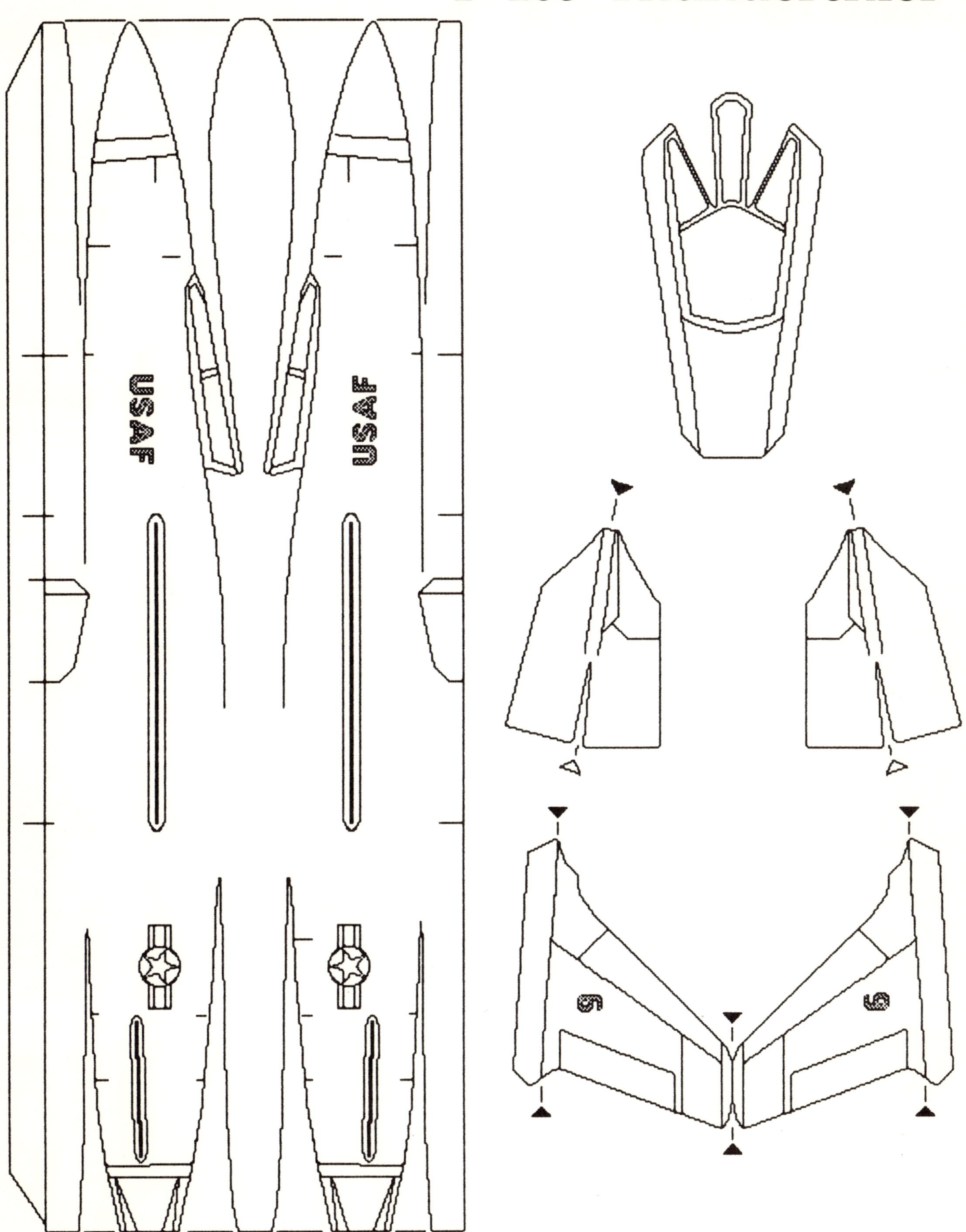

Etendard IU-M

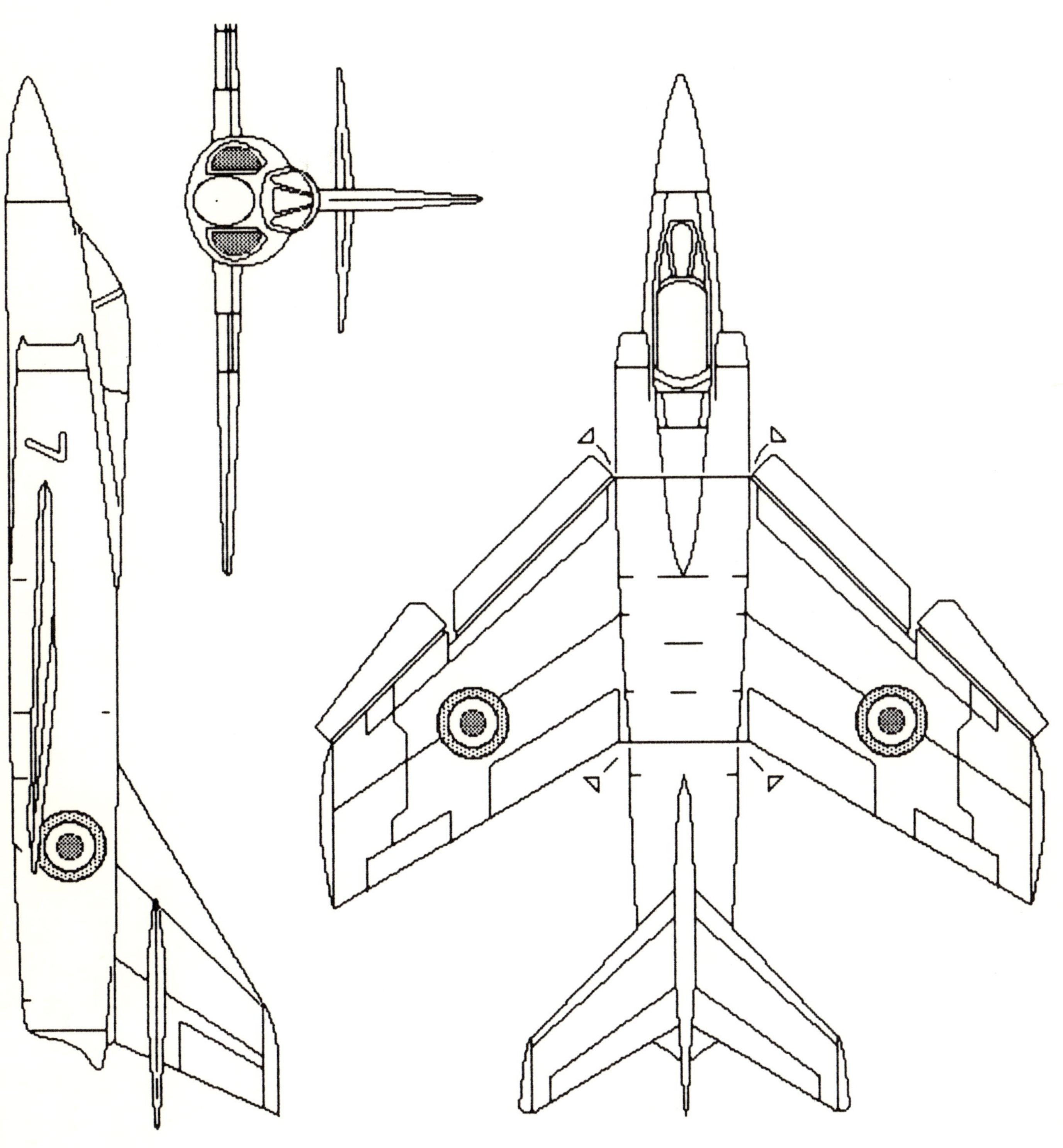

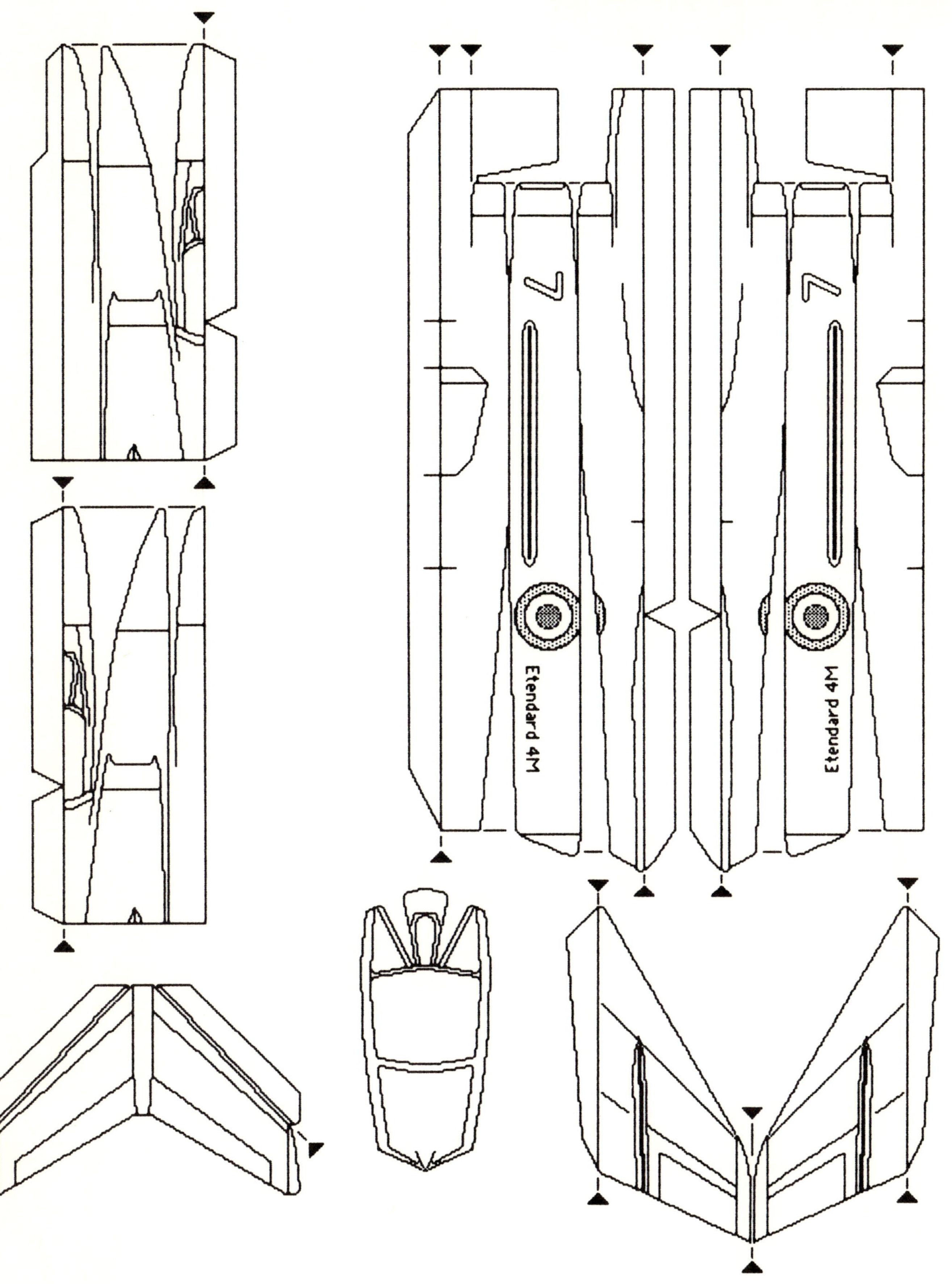

Etendard 4M
Etendard 4M

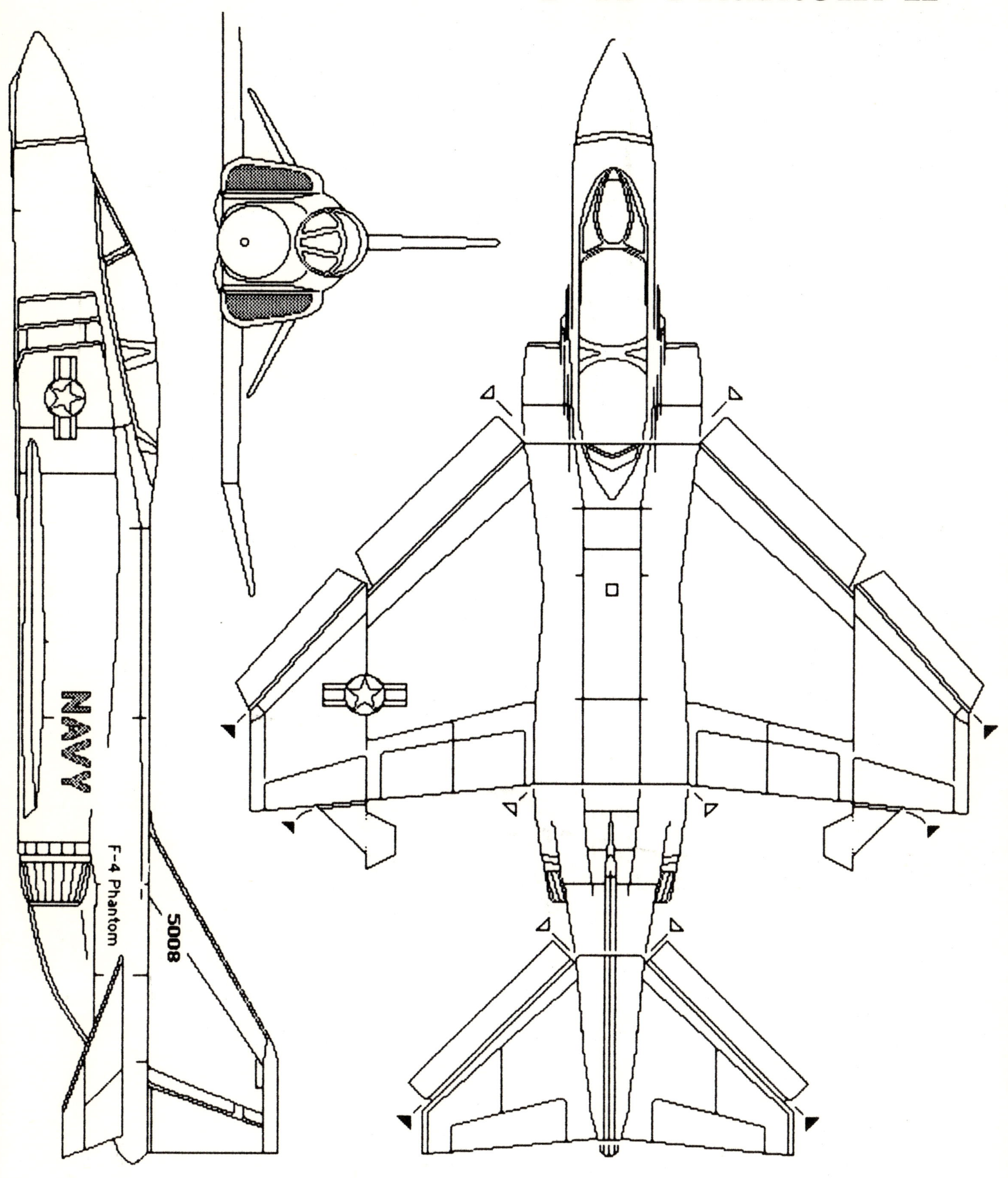

NAVY
F-4 Phantom
5008

F-4B Phantom II

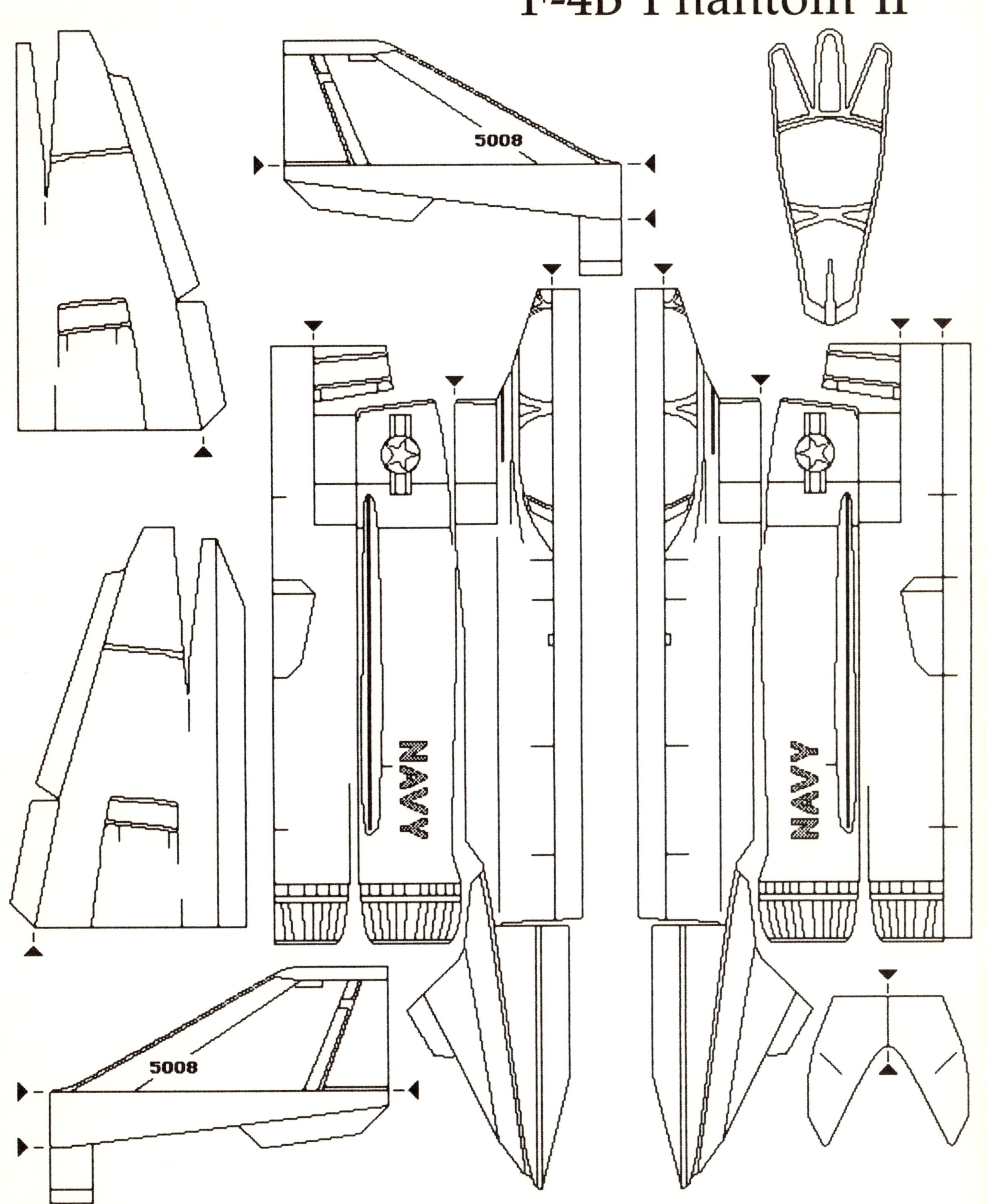

A-4E Skyhawk

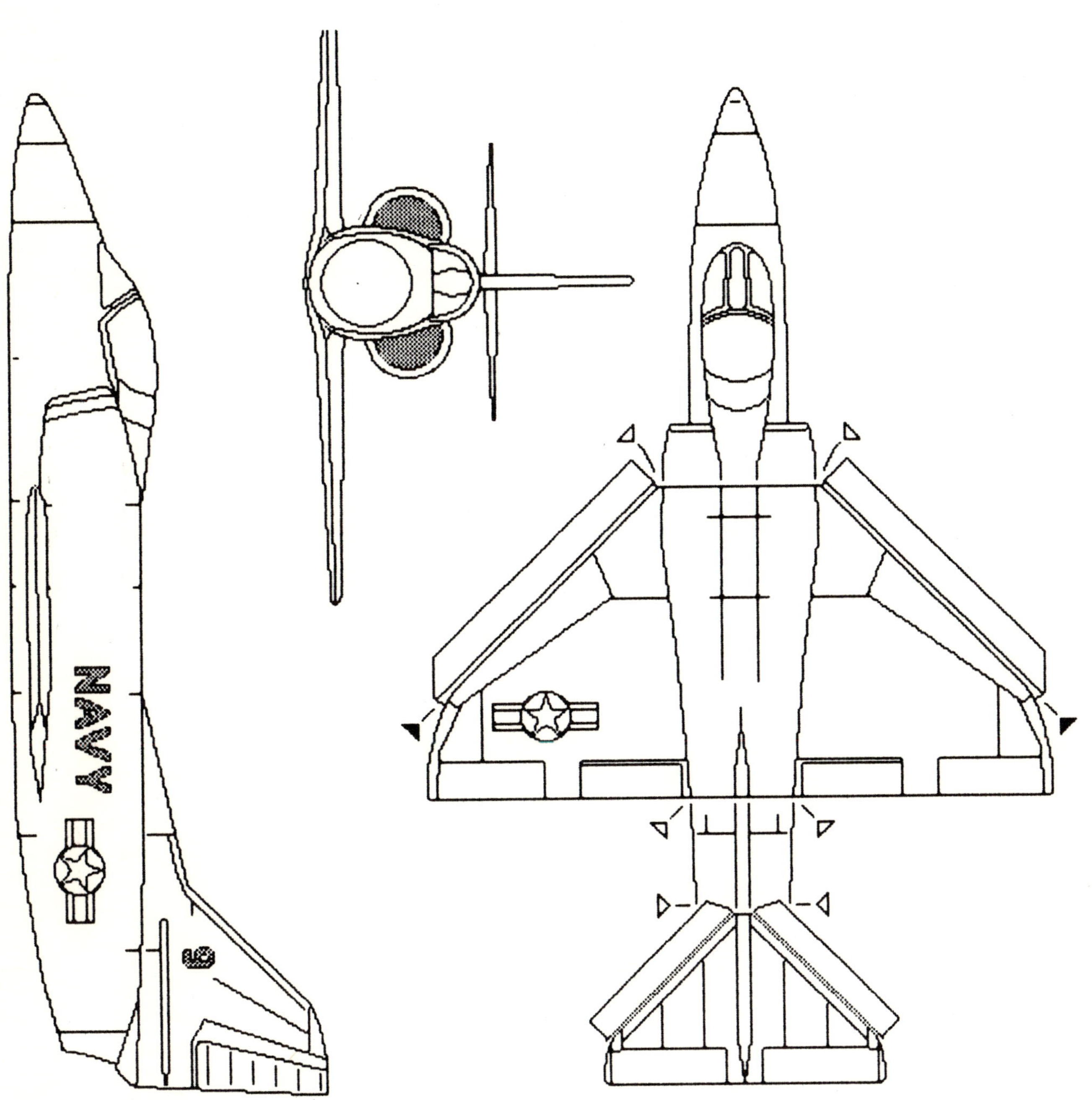

A-4E Skyhawk

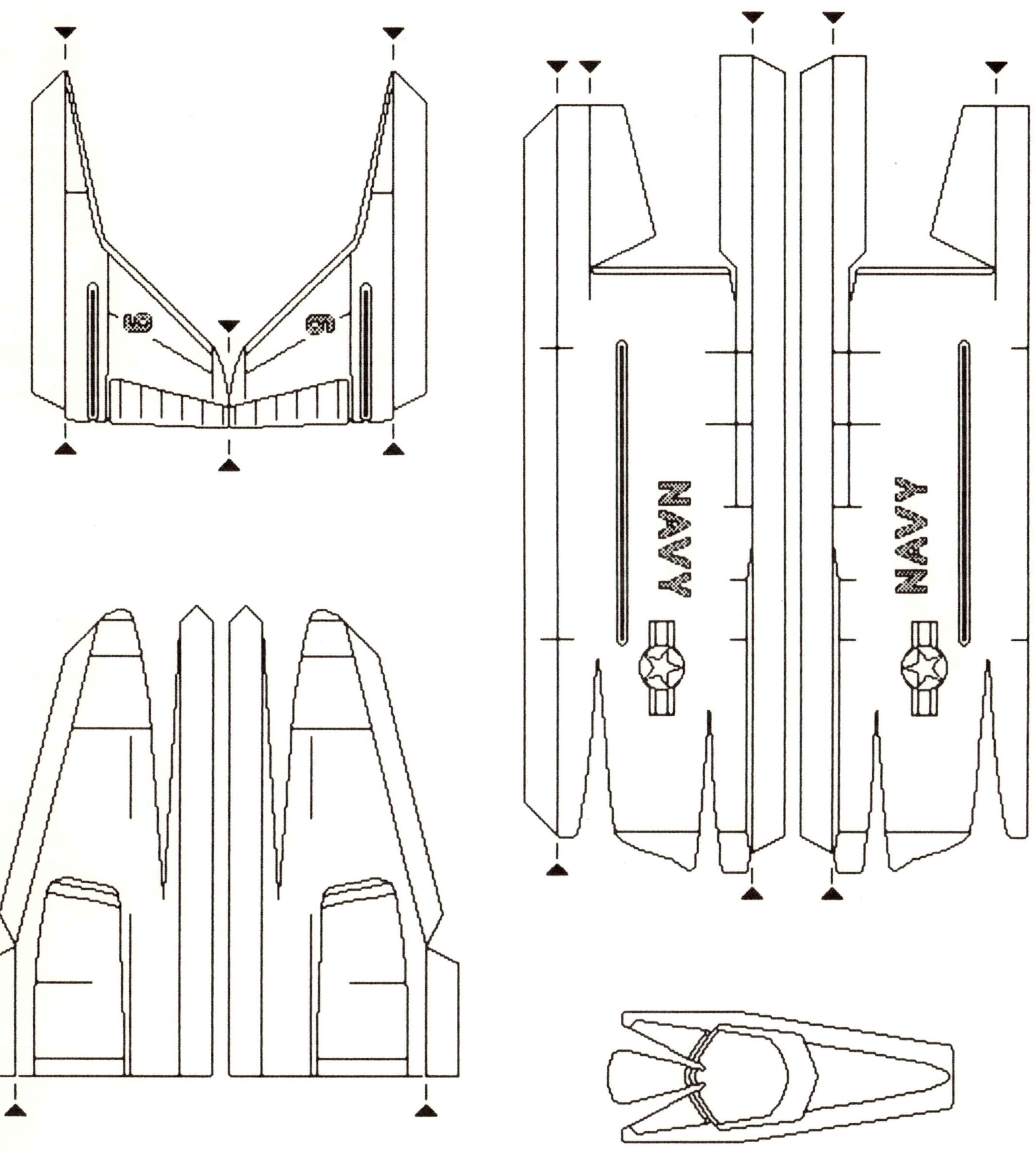

61